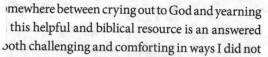

...mewhere between crying out to God and yearning ... this helpful and biblical resource is an answered ... both challenging and comforting in ways I did not know my spirit and soul needed. Her personal health journey provides a level of perception that only comes after someone has been refined by the fire. Come prepared to be ushered into moments of lavish grace, redeeming love, and freeing truth in *Closer Than Your Next Breath*.

Dr. Saundra Dalton-Smith, physician and author of *Sacred Rest*

I've gotten to know Susie Larson through radio conversations which, every time, soar, grace-soaked and drenched with power. Every conversation with Susie has made me more delighted in heart, more hopeful in spirit, and more in love with the Son of God. If you yearn for more conversations like that, read Susie's beautiful book, *Closer Than Your Next Breath*. It feels like an inspiring conversation with a cherished friend.

In an age of superficiality, Susie's insights run deep and lead readers into an authentic, fresh encounter with the living God. With relatable transparency, spot-on theology, and contagious warmth, Susie Larson's new book ushers readers into the throne room of grace to experience God's presence in real life.

Alan Wright, pastor, national radio teacher, and
best-selling author of *The Power to Bless*

How can God's presence be closer than your next breath? Because He already "is." His Spirit does not inhale—He IS always. Intimacy with Him is achieved by faith, the foundation of a present and eternally close relationship. Intimacy comes from a personal invitation to Holy Presence. Susie Larson opens and unpacks this supernatural concept noting that our souls do pant for God, as surely as a deer does for water. As we approach the most humble One in true humility, the One who died on the cross for us, this relationship grows. As we practice His presence, Jesus responds, which Susie clearly clarifies by the Word, reflections, prayer, and response/application. We secure our focus as we cease wandering, finding home in Presence, which is really closer than our next breath. Walking this out daily overcomes stagnant living through faith. The poignant illustration of being planted and letting the roots sink down into Him brings vision fueled by and founded on faith. I highly recommend exploring in Susie's writing God's work in your heart, an eternal relationship, now and forever.

Tom Phillips, Senior Advisor, Billy Graham Evangelistic Association

Susie's warm and wise voice is exactly what so many people need. In *Closer Than Your Next Breath*, she writes as a wise, empathetic friend; one who never judges us but points us to the real peace we're all looking for.

Brant Hansen, radio host and bestselling author of *Unoffendable*, *Blessed are the Misfits*, and *Life is Hard, God is Good, Let's Dance*

Closer Than Your Next Breath approaches the topic of God's presence in a manner that is both tactful and artful. Read and see how long it takes for Susie to sweep you into wistful wondering about the nature of our awesome God whose nearness is impossible to overstate.

Kyle Idleman, senior pastor of Southeast Christian Church and author of *When Your Way Isn't Working*

Susie Larson is a consistent voice of hope and truth. She courageously reminds all who listen that God is faithful and present. Her latest book, *Closer Than Your Next Breath*, is a valuable reminder that our circumstances do not alter God's promises. Susie invites the reader to a place of trust and courage. It is an important message in a season of great confusion. Susie has given the church a gift; I pray many will read and listen to God with new attention.

Allen Jackson, senior pastor of World Outreach Church and founder of Allen Jackson Ministries

What a breathtaking book from one of the wisest women I know, Susie Larson. If you're doubting, hungry, scared, or lonely, get this book. It will speak the hope of Jesus to your soul.

Lisa Whittle, Bible teacher, podcast host, and author of *God Knows*

CLOSER THAN YOUR NEXT

Breath

CLOSER THAN YOUR NEXT
Breath

WHERE IS GOD WHEN
YOU NEED HIM MOST?

SUSIE LARSON

W PUBLISHING GROUP

AN IMPRINT OF THOMAS NELSON

Published in Nashville, Tennessee, by W Publishing, an imprint of Thomas Nelson.

Author represented by The Steve Laube Agency.

Thomas Nelson titles may be purchased in bulk for educational, business, fundraising, or sales promotional use. For information, please email SpecialMarkets@ ThomasNelson.com.

Unless otherwise noted, Scripture quotations are taken from the Holy Bible, New Living Translation. Copyright © 1996, 2004, 2015 by Tyndale House Foundation. Used by permission of Tyndale House Ministries, Carol Stream, Illinois 60188. All rights reserved.

Scripture quotations marked AMP are taken from the Amplified® Bible (AMP). Copyright © 2015 by The Lockman Foundation. Used by permission. www.Lockman.org.

Scripture quotations marked MSG are taken from THE MESSAGE. Copyright © 1993, 2002, 2018 by Eugene H. Peterson. Used by permission of NavPress. All rights reserved. Represented by Tyndale House Publishers, a Division of Tyndale House Ministries.

Scripture quotations marked NIV are taken from the Holy Bible, New International Version®, NIV®. Copyright © 1973, 1978, 1984, 2011 by Biblica, Inc.® Used by permission of Zondervan. All rights reserved worldwide. www.zondervan.com. The "NIV" and "New International Version" are trademarks registered in the United States Patent and Trademark Office by Biblica, Inc.®

Scripture quotations marked NKJV are taken from the New King James Version®. Copyright © 1982 by Thomas Nelson. Used by permission. All rights reserved.

Scripture quotations marked THE VOICE are taken from *The Voice*™. Copyright © 2012 by Ecclesia Bible Society. Used by permission. All rights reserved. Italics appear in original.

Italics added to Scripture quotations (except THE VOICE quotations) are the author's emphasis.

Any internet addresses, phone numbers, or company or product information printed in this book are offered as a resource and are not intended in any way to be or to imply an endorsement by Thomas Nelson, nor does Thomas Nelson vouch for the existence, content, or services of these sites, phone numbers, companies, or products beyond the life of this book.

ISBN 978-0-7852-9467-2 (audiobook)
ISBN 978-0-7852-9466-5 (ePub)
ISBN 978-0-7852-9465-8 (SC)

Library of Congress Control Number

2023931874

Printed in the United States of America

23 24 25 26 27 LBC 6 5 4 3 2

To Esther, Karna, Melissa, Rebecca, Maria,
Tami, Sue, Kelli, and Tiffani,
for your bold, persistent, faith-filled
prayers. I'm healing because of you.

And to Lynn,
who's been fighting alongside and for us from the beginning.
May the Lord Himself replenish and restore all
you poured out for my family and me.

Contents

Where can I go from Your Spirit?

Or where can I flee from Your presence?

If I ascend into heaven, You are there;

If I make my bed in hell, behold, You are there.

If I take the wings of the morning,

And dwell in the uttermost parts of the sea,

Even there Your hand shall lead me,

And Your right hand shall hold me.

If I say, "Surely the darkness shall fall on me,"

Even the night shall be light about me;

Indeed, the darkness shall not hide from You,

But the night shines as the day;

The darkness and the light are both alike to You.

For You formed my inward parts;

You covered me in my mother's womb.

I will praise You, for I am fearfully and wonderfully made;

Marvelous are Your works,

And that my soul knows very well.

PSALM 139:7–14 NKJV

Introduction

God Is Here

Scripture tells us that God is omnipresent—He's present here, there, and everywhere, *all at the same time.* He dwells in the valley of the shadow[1] with the struggling soul. He's on top of the mountain with a triumphant soul. He's at the bedside of the one about to transition into glory, and He's at the soccer game of the young teen who struggles with identity issues.

I've heard people say, "God doesn't care where you park, where you eat, or where you work, for that matter. Just do those things as unto Him!" I couldn't disagree more. God cares deeply about every detail of your life. He's indifferent about *nothing.* He knows about the hurts in your heart and the hairs on your head.[2] He's in charge of every galaxy, and He has named every star in the sky. Ponder this reality for a moment.

The Lord God knows your limits, and He's aware of when you're pushed beyond them. He's near and far. He's up close and involved, and His glory fills the universe. Our God is unrivaled. God is God, and He is good. God is kind, faithful, strong, and trustworthy. He's just and righteous, meticulous and miraculous. God smiles and sings over us as His children.[3] He guards and guides, delivers and defends.

These things are true about God, and they compel us to praise Him, yes?

So why don't they always feel true? And if God is intimately involved in our lives, why does He allow us to suffer sometimes in unimaginable ways? If He can always intervene, why doesn't He? Where is God when we need Him most?

Though we often recognize God's involvement in our lives in hindsight, it's in the present where we learn to trust Him. It's in His presence where we're transformed to be like Him. Yet how do we process the intense suffering in our world? Why does God seem to wait so long to intervene when corruption and injustice run rampant?

These are questions too big for us to answer on this side of heaven. There's no way for us to live with peace and joy and a sense of holy expectancy unless we're also willing to embrace the mysteries of God. He's beyond understanding. His ways are higher than our ways, and His thoughts are higher than our thoughts.[4] Yet He's made Himself available to us. He's given us access to His throne room.[5] And He invites us to enter His gates not as cowering slaves but as worshiping, grateful, joyful saints who live assured that He's always glad to see us.

Though we can't fully explain suffering on this side of heaven, we can be assured that God has set a limit to our battles. He keeps the devil on a short leash. He fully intends to redeem every part of our story, to work all things together for the good of those of us who love Him and are called according to His purposes.[6] Knowing God is ever-present in our lives brings assurance to our souls. Sensing God's presence reminds us that we're made for another world.

My life verse is Psalm 116:9: "And so I walk in the LORD's presence as I live here on earth!"

What Is God's Presence?

What *is* the presence of God? Christians often talk about "seeking God's presence" or praying for God "to be present with us in this place." But what exactly does that mean?

The Bible says that it's in God's presence that we find the *fullness of joy.*[7] And the joy of the Lord is our strength, our superpower. It's in God's presence where we receive correction, direction, comfort, and assurance. God's presence brings clarity to our confusion, hope in place of despair.

In this book, we'll examine why God's presence is everything to us. We'll explore the surprising ways He shows up in our stories. We'll ponder seasons of silence and what we can learn from them. We'll look to Scripture to learn more about God's will and His ways with His people.

God is not subject to our formulas. He won't fit in our boundaries or boxes. He's not limited by our small thinking. His ways are higher, His thoughts are deeper, and His love is far greater than our minds can fathom.[8] His Spirit moves like the wind, and we're wise to catch sail when He breathes fresh life into us.

Though His presence is wonderful, it's not always understandable. If God is everywhere, all the time, why do some feel His presence more often than others? And what difference does the presence of God make in our lives today if we can't feel Him?

If every good gift comes from God, is "feeling good" the same as "feeling God"? When the worship team hits a chord progression that makes everyone want to raise their hands, is that God? Might it be for some but not for others?

There's nothing like God's presence. Maybe that's why we sometimes chase the sensational but miss the supernatural. We want to experience again what we experienced then. But in the process, might we rush right by the nuanced, miraculous ways God is showing up in our stories?

Christians sometimes say it's unbiblical to ask for more of God's presence because He's omnipresent. He's already here, there, and everywhere. Yet what about the psalms that cry out for more of God? And what about the verses that speak of God's movement? When God intervenes in the affairs of men, everything changes. He sometimes draws near. Other times He distances Himself. Why? And what about His movement in your life? He occasionally lifts you up. Other times He tucks you in. Sometimes He establishes you. Other times He hides you.

Let's agree that God's presence isn't a static, unmoving entity stuck in inertia. His presence is a force. It's powerful, moving, flowing, and breathing life into all creation.

God Reveals His Presence to Us

When God made Himself known in the Old Testament, even the most righteous souls were at once terrified. Though they sought hard after God, they were undone when they encountered Him.

In the New Testament, it's quite the same. Peter, James, and John saw Jesus transformed before their eyes. Jesus' face glowed like the sun, and His clothes became white as light. When God's voice thundered from heaven, the men fell facedown and were terrified.[9]

When the soldiers came to arrest Jesus and He asked who they were looking for, they said, "Jesus the Nazarene." Jesus stepped forward and said, "I AM he." And the sheer power that flowed from those words knocked a large contingent of soldiers off their feet.[10] Jesus proved that they weren't taking His life; He was freely giving it.

God's presence is power. He has no rival. He is the strength of our hearts and our portion forever.[11] So why doesn't everyone long for more of His presence? When Jesus ministered healing and wholeness to the broken and hurting, some of the townspeople begged Him to stay, while others begged Him to leave. Why such different responses?

Can we chase the presence of God? Block the presence of God? Hinder His work in our lives? Or does God simply do what He intends to do when it's time?

I've noticed, too, in Scripture that whenever God revealed His majesty and power, people had to make a choice: to move toward God or away from Him. The fact that our star-breathing God looks upon this pebble of a planet and takes great care to know about every detail of our lives is invitation enough to seek Him in ways you and I never have before.

A Journey into God's Presence

Please join me on this journey as we pursue the heart of God, through the Word of God, that we might more clearly understand the presence of God. I'll share stories along the way of everyday people whose lives were impacted by the tangible presence of God, including my own.

With all my heart, I pray this journey awakens a new thirst and hunger within you to know the God who put the stars in place and who is, right now, writing a story with your life that will take your breath away.

one

God Walks Through Walls

Your Fears Don't Scare Him

We live at the intersection of two theologies, two realities. The faithfulness of God is pursuing us from the past. The sovereignty of God is setting us up for the future. We live at the intersection of so far so God, and the best is yet to come.

MARK BATTERSON

The lawyer leaned in and gently asked me, "Did those boys shove you to the ground?" I blinked back a few tears and nodded yes. "Write it down." She continued, "Did they punch you?"

Once again, I wiped my eyes and whispered, "Yes."

She moved in a little closer and said, "What else? You said they pulled fistfuls of hair from your head. What else did they do to you? Write it down." I held the notepad to my chest, doubled over, and sobbed. I didn't think I could revisit that memory from so long ago.

Thankfully, this wasn't a literal deposition. God has surrounded me with fiery, praying women who are determined to see me free, healed, and whole. And they're not stopping until I'm completely free. Free from the chronic illness that has plagued me for more than three decades and free from childhood trauma that kept me bracing for impact. One of these women is a lawyer. Through both her legal work and her time in God's Word, she now teaches about the judicial nature of God and leads people through what she calls Mercy Trials to help them get free (we'll hear from her a little later in the book).

Years ago I sought counseling about the trauma I experienced as a child. Yet even though I'd forgiven the perpetrators, my body still hung on to the effects of sexual and physical assault. Bracing for impact was my default setting. I'd tried everything to get free: fasting, praying, memorizing Scripture, deep breathing, deep stretching, and so on. Those things served me well in my spiritual growth, but my body had been stuck in fight-or-flight mode until that day.

Our Experiences Imprint on Our Souls

They say nerves that fire together wire together. In other words, when something happens to us that affects us at a deep emotional level, that experience and the emotions around our experience leave an imprint within us at a cellular and neurological level. We may wonder why we're so triggerable. We wonder why certain reminiscent experiences ignite a disproportionate response in us. Excessive reactions often point to something within us that needs healing, truth, and redemption.

The good news is, we're not permanently damaged. God created our brains with a capacity for rewiring. He made our souls for restoration. One moment in God's presence—one word of revelation, insight, or direction—can do what we could never do over a lifetime for ourselves. Jesus offers us Himself to heal our souls, make us whole, save us from our sins, and make all things new again.

We're made for His presence. We have access to the inner throne room of Almighty God, who makes all things new.

> We're made for His presence. We have access to the inner throne room of Almighty God, who makes all things new.

Our loving Father often takes us back to certain parts of our stories—never leaving our sides for a moment—before He propels us forward into our next place of promise. We may not always feel His nearness, but He's intimately involved with every nuance of our lives. He helps us to re-story our story. He gives us new experiences and redemptive perspectives. His presence changes everything.

Consider for a moment a memory etched in the apostle Peter's physiology. Peter loved Jesus. Passionately so. Peter walked away from the life he knew to follow a Savior he barely knew.[1] Something about Jesus' presence captured this rough fisherman's heart. Imagine a day in their lives. Peter watched as Jesus approached a leper. Jesus embraced this ravaged soul, smiled, looked to heaven, and healed him. *Made new.* That's what the presence of God can do.

Peter stood awestruck, shook his head, and wondered where all this would take him. Finally, the Messiah had come!

But then, years later, things spun out of control. Evil eclipsed heaven. Peter forgot who he was. Forgot who Jesus was. In the face of terror, Peter's instinctive response wasn't a holy remembrance but a fearful reaction.

While Jesus faced His accusers, the town's bystanders warmed themselves by a charcoal fire. Peter tried to blend in. He wanted to know what would happen to his Savior and friend.

Others asked whether Peter followed the Savior. Jarred by the question, Peter denied it—three times. He even spewed out a few curse words from his former life.[2]

The devil condemningly tries to pull us into our past because he's terrified of what God has prepared for our future. God lovingly brings us back to our past so He can propel us into our future.

> The devil condemningly tries to pull us into our past because he's terrified of what God has prepared for our future. God lovingly brings us back to our past so He can propel us into our future.

Traumatic memories have a way of imprinting on our senses. Charcoal fires were the norm in biblical times. Picture Peter, days later, on a cold night, warming his hands by a fire. The wind shifted, and a puff of charcoal smoke blew in his face. He suddenly felt sick to his stomach, defeated and depressed. The memory of that horrible night returned with a force. He looked around to see whether anyone noticed the sweat on his temples. He shook off the memory but couldn't seem to shake the shame.

Our Enemy loves to re-create reminiscent experiences to

trigger and traumatize us. And it works—until God brings truth and healing to our souls.

Brain scientists often point to Jesus' purposeful intention of building a charcoal fire on the beach when He reappeared to Peter and the other disciples. Jesus knew that Peter's memory would forever haunt him without a God-encounter and a new experience around a charcoal fire. So Jesus initiated one.

The Messiah asked Peter three times, "Do you love me?"[3] Imagine how Peter must have felt. Hasty, impulsive, broken-hearted Peter. He was face-to-face with Jesus. Death couldn't hold Him. Peter's failure didn't stop Him.

Picture Jesus' eyes flooded with love, compassion, and understanding. He wasn't there to sentence Peter but to give him a new sensory experience. Not there to remind Peter of how he messed up but to recommission him. Peter needed a fresh encounter with God—one that eclipsed his traumatic memory and epic failure; one that restored and revived his faith. One that reminded Peter that God Almighty still wanted to use him to change the world. God has such encounters in mind for you as well.

Imagine the scene when Peter and John reached Jesus' tomb—only to find it was empty! John described their experience like this:

> Early on Sunday morning, while it was still dark, Mary Magdalene came to the tomb and found that the stone had been rolled away from the entrance. She ran and found Simon Peter and the other disciple, the one whom Jesus loved. She said, "They have taken the Lord's body out of the tomb, and we don't know where they have put him!"[4]

I love John's gospel. Well, I love all the Gospels, really. But there's something about how John described himself as "the disciple Jesus loved"[5] that endears me to him. I don't think he was implying that he was the one Jesus loved most of all but rather that Jesus' love changed everything for him. John's whole identity was wrapped up in the love of his Savior. I don't see this as prideful boasting. I think John encountered such intimacy and fellowship with his Messiah that he learned how to live loved. Jesus' love became the filter through which John saw the rest of his life. And as we encounter God's love in ever-increasing measures, we, too, will begin to see ourselves and the world with new eyes.

Still, I laugh out loud every time I read the account of how Peter and John raced to the tomb, because John found it essential to mention that *he* won the race.[6] I think I would have included that detail as well.

I imagine that after young John reached the tomb, he leaned against the rock, put his hand on his stomach, and heaved heavy breaths as he waited for the older Peter to arrive. He noticed the linen wrappings lying inside the tomb but didn't go inside. Peter sprinted onto the scene and came to a jarring halt. He also saw the linens and decided to be the first inside the tomb.

Consider where these two men stood for a moment. The tomb was a place of trauma for Jesus' followers. It's where their dreams came crashing down around them with such finality it would take an act of God to resurrect them.

John—who identified himself as someone deeply loved by God—said that he saw the *empty* tomb and *believed*.[7] Wait, what? *John, don't you wonder where they put the body? What if someone stole it? Moved it? Disposed of it?* My spiritual gift of suspicion is going bonkers right now.

Scripture says that John and Peter hadn't understood Jesus' promise until the moment He rose from the grave.[8] But the empty tomb was enough for them. Wow. They walked so closely with their Savior and friend that they didn't need all the answers—just a glimpse of glory now and then.

It's thought that after Mary went to tell the disciples about the empty tomb, she likely went to tell others. That's why Peter and John were at the tomb alone. They must have departed before she returned to the tomb, because Scripture tells us that she stood once more outside the tomb, put her face in her hands, and wept. This dear woman, once tormented by demons, was forever free because of Jesus. She followed Jesus, supported His ministry, and learned daily from Him. Imagine her heartbreak when they crucified Him. *But this was a new day.* When she finally looked inside the tomb, she saw a fantastic sight.

Mary was standing outside the tomb crying, and as she wept, she stooped and looked in. She saw two white-robed angels, one sitting at the head and the other at the foot of the place where the body of Jesus had been lying. "Dear woman, why are you crying?" the angels asked her.

"Because they have taken away my Lord," she replied, "and I don't know where they have put him."[9]

Bible scholars marvel at this moment, especially considering the ark of the covenant. Search online for a picture of the ark of the covenant and you'll find an elaborate gold structure with two angels mounted on top—one on the right, the other on the left. The space in between is known as the mercy seat, which represents where and how the law was given to Moses.

Under the new covenant, the mercy seat takes on a whole new meaning. Jesus is the fulfillment of the law. *He* is our mercy seat! Nothing is a coincidence with God.

Try to imagine the scene when Mary peeked inside the empty tomb. Doesn't it take your breath away to consider that inside the tomb—inside the place where it seemed death had won the day—we're given a glimpse of the ark of the *new* covenant? Mary saw an angel at the foot and an angel at the head of the place where Jesus once lay, and in the space between she saw Jesus' robe—the area known as the mercy seat. What extravagant love! That God would reveal such a prophetic wonder to Mary, one who would no doubt wonder about her worth after Jesus' death, reveals how intimately acquainted He is with every one of us.

Consider God's tender and personal care for Peter and Mary. God gave Peter a charcoal-fire experience to recommission him and remind him, "You think your badness has disqualified you, but it's My goodness that qualifies you. I love you. I know you love Me. Now, go and preach the good news." And to sweet Mary, who likely in the days ahead doubted God's full redemptive work in her life, God gave a divine glimpse into the finished work of Christ!

Here's another beautiful twist in the story. The angels at Jesus' empty tomb asked Mary why she was crying. I think they knew, don't you? "Because they have taken away my Lord," she replied, "and I don't know where they have put him."[10] She turned to leave and almost bumped into the gardener. It was Jesus, but He appeared in such a simple way that she almost missed Him. Maybe I'm speculating a bit too much here, but I wonder if Jesus appeared as a gardener to remind her that He came for those the rest of the world finds easy to disregard, because she was one such person. Yet as soon as Jesus said her name, she recognized her Savior!

God's Presence Brings Peace

John's gospel tells us that later that evening, the disciples were hiding behind locked doors because they were afraid. Suddenly, Jesus stood there among them. "Peace be with you," He said to them.[11] As He spoke, He opened His hands so they could see His wounds and pulled back His robe so they could see the scar in His side. What was that like? The disciples were overjoyed! They went from fear to faith in a few seconds. There's a common saying that we're always only ten seconds away from an emotional ditch, but I'd say we're only ten seconds away from mountain-moving faith. Encountering God changes everything.

Jesus walked through their fear-walls and met them right in the middle of their terror and trauma. He fiercely loves us that way, you know? I think we've misjudged the Lion of Judah. In Revelation 3:20, we read about how Jesus stands at the door and knocks and waits for us to open the door. We've somehow interpreted it to mean that He passively waits for us to tear down all the walls we've built, all the doors we've locked, and all the systems we've put in place to self-protect.

> We're only ten seconds away from mountain-moving faith. Encountering God changes everything.

But there's not a passive bone in Jesus' body. Indeed, He'll never force anyone to follow Him. But make no mistake about it, He's on a rescue mission and will cross hell and high water to get to us. He doesn't just pursue us to save us. That's, of course, His primary mission.[12] But goodness and mercy chase after us all the days of our lives because our Healer loves us. Look in

Scripture at all the barriers Jesus crossed to get to people who seemed unredeemable.[13]

We'll explore both the fierceness and gentleness of God in future chapters, but for now, let's continue looking at the story in John 20. The disciples were hiding behind locked doors. Jesus walked through the walls and surprised His followers with a greeting of peace. He showed them His wounds and then commissioned and empowered them: "'As the Father has sent me, so I am sending you.' Then he breathed on them and said, 'Receive the Holy Spirit.'"[14]

There's more to this part of the story, but I want to jump down to the part where Scripture tells us that Thomas was absent when Jesus appeared to the disciples. Picture Thomas's friends waving their arms, talking over one another, and trying to get their words out faster than their brains allowed: "Jesus is alive! He showed up here! He gave us an assignment! The story is not over! Jesus lives!"

How did Thomas respond? He refused to believe unless he saw the Lord for himself and touched His wounds with his own bare hands. People sometimes call him "doubting Thomas." But might he be "hurting Thomas"? Or "traumatized Thomas"? Just because someone's faith doesn't come as easily or quickly as others' doesn't make them a substandard Christian. It may mean that they need certain kinds of experiences with God others don't. An empty tomb was enough for John to believe. But not for Thomas.

So how did Jesus respond to Thomas's doubt? John 20:26 tells us that He showed up *again*, eight days later. Then Jesus put His hands on His hips, cursed Thomas, and kicked him out of the group. *Not!* Thank the Lord. No, Jesus appeared to His disciples, walked through the walls again, and pronounced a blessing of peace (not a curse of rejection or disappointment). Then Jesus approached Thomas and invited him to touch His wounds. He told Thomas to no longer be faithless but to believe. Thomas was undone. He blurted out, "My Lord and my God!"[15] Jesus replied, "You believe because you have seen me. Blessed are those who believe without seeing me."[16]

Though there's mercy from the heart of God when we struggle to believe, there is a special blessing of favor when we find room in our hearts to believe. The word "blessed" Jesus used in verse 29 speaks of happy feelings that come from being favored by God.[17] Whether this feels true or not, it is true: we have a heavenly Father who will cross every barrier to help us heal, that we might more fiercely trust Him and believe.

We live in the tension of pain and hurt, which dims our view of God and the wonder of our experiences with a far kinder God than we ever imagined Him to be. If we live suspicious of His goodness, we may miss His goodness when it comes. But make no mistake about it: His goodness has come and is coming.

> Surely your goodness and unfailing love will pursue me all the days of my life, and I will live in the house of the LORD forever.
>
> PSALM 23:6

God's Presence Heals

You've no doubt experienced trauma of your own. God wants to heal those places in your story and restore you. And you likely have experiences from your childhood that you've misinterpreted. Maybe the closed door you faced wasn't rejection but rather God's protection. There were likely times when your soul felt traumatized by danger only to learn that the threat wasn't as real as you believed it to be.

The Enemy of your soul doesn't care about the difference between real trauma and misinterpreted experiences; he just wants your heartache to hold you captive. Thankfully, you have a fierce advocate in Jesus,[18] who intends to lead you into all truth so that you can be truly, sincerely, profoundly free.

> When the Spirit of truth comes, he will guide you into all truth. He will not speak on his own but will tell you what he has heard. He will tell you about the future.
>
> JOHN 16:13

Mark Batterson joins me on my radio show occasionally. He said something (and this is my paraphrase) that I'm still thinking about: "Sometimes we need new experiences. And sometimes we need better explanations."

It's amazing how a redemptive perspective can change your day (and your health). Sometimes God brings us back to a memory so He can give us a more redemptive interpretation. And sometimes He provides new experiences that eclipse and help heal our painful memories. If you follow Jesus, if you enjoy His presence and respond to His voice, then you're already on the path of healing and transformation.

*This is a good life—my heart is
glad, my soul is full of joy,
and my body is at rest.
Who could want for more?
You will not abandon me to
experience death and the grave
or leave me to rot alone.
Instead, You direct me on the path
that leads to a beautiful life.
As I walk with You, the pleasures are never-ending,
and I know true joy and contentment.*

PSALM 16:9–11 (THE VOICE)

Reflect

1. Read through John 20–21 and note the various supernatural moments you find in these chapters.[19] How many did you count, and what was God's purpose (as best you can discern) for each of these encounters?
2. Of the supernatural encounters you found in John 20–21,

which one means the most to you or most stands out to you? Why?

3. We all get distracted in different ways. What's one thing in your life that continually pulls your gaze away from God?

4. Sit with the Lord a bit. Ask the Holy Spirit to lead you into all truth. What's behind this distraction? What's God's remedy for you? Wait. Listen. Write down what you sense the Lord saying to you.

Pray

Father in heaven, holy is Your name. Your kingdom come. Your will be done on earth (and in me) as it is in heaven.[20] Thank You for the countless ways You guard and guide me, protect me, and provide for me. I want to know You more. I want my life to reflect Your power and Your glory. I long to understand all Jesus won for me at Calvary. Open my eyes where I'm blind. Unstop my ears where I'm deaf. Awaken my heart where I'm asleep. Ignite my passions for Your purpose for me. I want my life to count for all of eternity. Take me to the next place You have for me. In Jesus' matchless name I pray, amen.

Respond

Turn off your phone notifications before you go to bed. Turn on an instrumental playlist upon waking in the morning, push your phone aside, open your Bible in your lap, take a few deep breaths, sit quietly before the Lord, read His Word, and wait for Him to speak. Let His be the first voice you hear tomorrow (and the next day and the next).

Ponder His Presence

If I Chase the Sensational, Might I Miss the Supernatural?

We all long to see God move in our midst. When the Almighty breaks through our earthbound existence, we stand in awe. We suddenly realize that we're more spiritual than physical. We're made for another world, for the heavenly kingdom. We're never the same after a holy encounter with God. These moments light a fire in us if we are alive in Christ. Suddenly, our worldly passions fade, and eternity is all that matters.

Is it possible to miss the mark when our hearts burn so passionately for God? Unfortunately, it is. We veer off course when we only equate the sensational with the supernatural. Or when we think that signs and wonders can only happen in a hyped-up meeting. Just because we experienced God's presence a certain way in the past doesn't mean that's the only way He'll reveal Himself to us in the future.

God meets His children in countless ways throughout our

days. He is in the nooks and crannies of our everyday existence. He's with us in the morning when we're sipping on our coffee, and He's with us at night when we're tossing anxiously in bed. If we look for Him, we will find Him. But if we only look for Him in the sensational, we might miss Him.

Read these wise words from one of my study Bibles:

True spiritual fires dwindle 1) when we allow the excitement of the crowds and miracles to dull our ears to hearing the foundational truths of the Holy Spirit's counsel; 2) when we look to the visitation of the Spirit to shore up weaknesses in the local fellowship rather than correct the problems; 3) when we allow an attitude of pride and showmanship to distort the simplicity of God's workings and the visitation is reduced to a cleverly publicized event; 4) when we fail to maintain the balance of the pastoral needs of the congregation, substituting the sheer energy of the meetings for shepherd care and faithful feeding of the sheep; 5) when we neglect to make disciples, who would have multiplied the effectiveness of the revival; 6) when we allow breakdown of authority and unity in the leadership team through prayerlessness, weariness, or functioning outside the boundaries of individuals' giftings; 7) when we look to "professionals" to further the growth of the church, instead of fostering release of ministries that have bonded to the life and value system of the congregation; 8) when we lose the focus and object of loving worship by using "worship" as a means of stimulating desired responses in people; 9) when we allow the "busyness and excitement" of revival to take priority over vigilance in humble prayer and intercession.[1]

If we live from one spiritual high to the next, if we're constantly seeking supernatural revelation but not living up to what we already know, then we'll never mature.[2] And, unfortunately, we'll add to the stigma that some Christians are so heavenly minded that they're no earthly good. On the other side of that debate are Christians who proudly reject *any* movement of the Holy Spirit because they think they're somehow too dignified to long for Someone they don't understand or cannot control.

But let us remember that walking in God's presence involves moments when we can't sense Him, but we trust Him. It involves moments when He breaks through and we're forever changed. And walking intimately with God involves moments of honest-to-goodness obedience while we wait to see what He'll do next.

Prayer

Lord, I'm sorry for the times I've reduced our relationship to a series of emotional encounters and hyped-up events. You're so much more than that! You are a star-breathing God, and You hold my whole life in Your hands. There's never a moment when I don't have You. Help me to live increasingly aware of Your beautiful presence. Amen.

two

God Draws Near

His Presence Transforms You

Try taking long walks through the woods. Paint a picture no one else will see. Read the ancients by candlelight. Consider the stars at midnight. Wander through an art museum. Play the piano when only God can listen. Pick out a journal and take up a pen. Plant a garden and delight in dirt-covered hands. Resist rushing and seize the opportunity in hidden years to discover how you were uniquely designed to walk intimately with God.

ALICIA BRITT CHOLE

t was morning. I sat up in my bed, and my eyes fell upon the plaque I read every morning:

Happy. Healthy. Holy. Healed.

This simple shiplap plaque sits on the floor, leaned against the wall, so it's the first thing I see when I slip out of bed onto my knees at the start of each new day. I usually glance at the words, close my eyes, open my hands, and whisper a prayer something like this: "Glorify Your name in and through me, Lord. You are my Savior, Deliverer, Healer, and Friend. You're my Banner, my Victory, my Defender, and my Peace. I possess all in You. Do a mighty work in me."

I love my little work of art because it lists the things that I'm believing God for, things I'm still possessing in ever-deepening ways. Author and pastor Scotty Smith said this on my radio show a while back, and I'm still thinking about it: "We've underestimated the power of the good news. There's nothing more than the gospel. And there's so much more to the gospel." Exactly and amen!

Happy. Healthy. Holy. Healed.

Happy: You thrill me, LORD, with all you have done for me! I sing for joy because of what you have done. O LORD, what great works you do! And how deep are your thoughts. (Psalm 92:4–5)

Healthy: Dear friend, I hope all is well with you and that you are as healthy in body as you are strong in spirit. (3 John v. 2)

Holy: For by that one offering he forever made perfect those who are being made holy. (Hebrews 10:14)

Healed: But he was pierced for our rebellion, crushed for our sins. He was beaten so we could be whole. He was whipped so we could be healed. (Isaiah 53:5)

So Much More

If through Jesus' victory on the cross He won us an ocean, we've grasped only the water we can hold in our hands. There's so much more to God's presence than our minds can comprehend. His promises are so much more potent than we can ever imagine. His character is unshakable, and His faithfulness is immovable. He means what He says and will do what He's promised. There's much more to His involvement in the world and in our lives than our often-skewed perspective allows. There's no end to His understanding, no boundaries to His compassion, and no limit to the love He has for His children.

If we spend the rest of our lives following, fellowshipping, and fiercely believing what God says, we'll grasp something of His goodness and grace, which will change everything for us. And what remains? So much more! The glory, majesty, authority, sovereignty, and power of our star-breathing God, who takes delight in fellowshipping with *us*. Imagine.

After a three-decade-long battle with Lyme disease, I always know within five minutes how I'm going to feel each day, with only a few exceptions. Occasionally I'll perk up even if the day

> If we spend the rest of our lives following, fellowshipping, and fiercely believing what God says, we'll grasp something of His goodness and grace, which will change everything for us. And what remains? So much more!

started rough. But most times—at least as it relates to my health and energy level—my physical health is largely dependent upon the night before. If I sleep well, I wake up with a spring in my step even though the inflammatory symptoms hide in the shadows and surge at unexpected times. I can deal with a lot if I can just get some sleep.

If I don't sleep well, I wake up with a numb neck and face, blurred vision, head pressure, and an automatically discouraged soul. Sadly, discouragement has been a default response and a battlefield for me (until recently, but that's for another chapter).

This was one such morning. I sat up and immediately slouched, opened my hands, and closed my heavy eyelids. I breathed a heavy sigh and slipped out of my bed and onto my knees. I couldn't help myself; I cried out to God, "Oh, Lord, how long? How long until You rescue me from this wretched disease? Why can't I win this battle? What's holding me back? Is there anything else You want from me? Anything else I'm missing? If I'm honest, I feel hurt by You. I don't understand why I hear Your voice in some areas of my life but not this one. Why aren't You moving? Why aren't You speaking?"

Nothing. No sense of God's presence. No response. Just an inflamed body and a discouraged soul.

I padded out to the kitchen and grabbed my supplements, vitamin drink, and the one cup of coffee I allow myself every morning. You could say I'm hypervigilant to a fault (again, until recently, but I'll explain later). My eyes downcast, I sat, cradled my mug, and felt the nudge to look up. I was all at once breathless. The sky was ablaze with color and majesty. A masterpiece.

My entire body tingled, but not in an inflammatory way—*in the way of presence*. I felt God's nearness. I sensed His immense love for me. His abounding grace—and without a hint of condemnation. This was a holy moment.

Bright orange and deep pink, mixed with swirls of white clouds and blue skies, created a display that stunned me. I had just dragged my feet out of my bedroom with grumbling on my lips. And what did God do? He overwhelmed me with a work of art, simply because He is God. That's who He is. That's how He is.

But it wasn't just the sky canvas that humbled me. The sun looked especially big that morning. Like it had moved unnaturally close, or should I say, *super*naturally close, right up in my face. The sun blazed with such size and force that I held my breath. Then, with head bowed in humble surrender, I whispered, "Daily, the heavens pour forth speech.[1] *God, You are always speaking. May I always be listening.*"

Without taking my eyes off the sky, I set aside my mug. I slipped out of my chair onto my knees and cried out, "Oh, God! I know You welcome the laments of my heart; You invite me to be honest with You. But Lord, forgive me for accusing You of not being there for me. You're here! Always with me! Always involved. You will never leave me nor forsake me. I put my trust in You."

Spiritual Receptivity

In his book *The Pursuit of God*, A.W. Tozer wrote about a time when he felt curious as to why—if God is no respecter of persons[2]—some go on to do great things for God while others live stuck in their circumstances. If we serve the same God, have the same Holy Spirit at work within us, and have the same promises to stand on, then why such discrepancy?

Tozer's discovery fascinated me. He searched history and considered some of the great Christians who've gone before us, only to learn that their differences couldn't be starker. Some were rich, while some were poor. Some were Black, and some White. Some were educated; some were not. But he did find one common denominator among them all. They possessed what Tozer called *spiritual receptivity*.

> Something in them was open to heaven, something which urged them Godward. Without attempting anything like a profound analysis, I shall say simply that they had spiritual awareness and that they went on to cultivate it until it became the biggest thing in their lives. They differed from the average person in that when they felt the inward longing, *they did something about it*. They acquired a lifelong habit of spiritual response.[3]

What might a *habit of spiritual response* look like for you and me? Do we respond differently to God when we sense His presence and when we don't? I sure have. I'm saddened at the thought of it. Is He the same God when He seems silent? Is He still holding the universe together? Still intervening in the affairs of men? Still showing mercy and grace toward us when we least deserve it? Still *actively* answering prayers, even though we were crabby yesterday and we're behind on our task list today?

He is the same God whether we can sense Him or not! He's still moving on our behalf, using every aspect of our lives as an invitation to know Him more and experience Him in a way that transforms us. If we believe that His Word is true and that we can never get away from His presence, then we know He's worthy of our worship, praise, and gratitude no matter what our senses and momentary experiences tell us. A glorious eternity awaits us. Our time on earth is not a placeholder or time killer until the real party starts. Jesus won a sound victory so we could possess some of our inheritance now while we wait for its fulfillment.

Our trials and triumphs are packed with opportunities that impact eternity. Daily, God gives us opportunities to shift our weight onto His promises and discover that they hold. How we steward all Jesus won for us ripples out around us and echoes into eternity.

As we draw near to God, He draws near to us.[4] I don't know who said it first, but it's been said that "you can have as much of God as you want." When He graces you with a tangible expression of His presence, you acquire a hunger and a thirst for the things of God. You begin to run with purpose in every step. And the chase changes you. You begin to throw off everything that hinders you and deal ruthlessly with thoughts that weaken or derail you. You learn to fix your eyes on Jesus.[5]

You learn to live in a way that conveys God's heart for the world. You become someone of the kingdom. You know to rely on God's promises more than you do your circumstances. You actively look for reasons to be grateful, and you're quick to notice the new life springing up all around you. You don't let the storm shake you; you shake the storm because you're anchored to Christ.

> Our trials and triumphs are packed with opportunities that impact eternity. Daily, God gives us opportunities to shift our weight onto His promises and discover that they hold.

When we're attentive to His presence and responsive to His voice, heaven's influence comes to earth, and God's message of redemption echoes through us and reverberates into our culture. I would dare say that the more we cultivate a lifestyle of listening and response, the sharper our spiritual senses become to His movement all around us.

> For our present troubles are small and won't last very long. Yet they produce for us a glory that vastly outweighs them and will last forever! So we don't look at the troubles we can see now; rather, we fix our gaze on things that cannot be seen. For the things we see now will soon be gone, but the things we cannot see will last forever.[6]

The Earth Is Filled with His Glory!

The sun is at the center of the solar system. The sun's surface heat exceeds ten thousand degrees. If you try to get up close and personal with the sun, you're done. One day, during one of my deep-thought moments, I pondered the sun's heat and the fact that God merely spoke and the heavens came to be. Read this powerful passage:

> The LORD merely spoke,
> and the heavens were created.
> He breathed the word,
> and all the stars were born.
> He assigned the sea its boundaries
> and locked the oceans in vast reservoirs.

Let the whole world fear the LORD,
and let everyone stand in awe of him.
For when he spoke, the world began!
It appeared at his command.[7]

This God of ours—the one who loves us with intense passion and meticulous attention to detail—*this God merely spoke, and the heavens came to be*. It makes me cry out with the psalmist, "What is man that You are mindful of him?"[8]

Why is it that if we draw near to the sun we'll burn up, but we can draw intimately near to the One who made the sun and not be destroyed? In fact, amazingly, the opposite is true. When we draw near to Him, our soul finds its home, our heart finds its rest, and our story finds redemption. If Scripture says that our God is a consuming fire, why are we not consumed when we draw near? I found the answer in the book of Lamentations:

Because of the LORD's great love we are not consumed,
for his compassions never fail.
They are new every morning;
great is your faithfulness.
I say to myself, "The LORD is my portion;
therefore I will wait for him."
The LORD is good to those whose hope is in him,
to the one who seeks him.[9]

We can draw intimately near to the One who made the sun because of the way He is. It's because of *His love* we are not consumed. His mercies are new every morning. His fire consumes everything in and around us that destroys the life of God within us. Jesus came to destroy the works of the devil. Whether we wake up crabby or spring out of bed, He's always the same, pouring out His mercies, establishing us in His grace, and inviting us continually to seek His face.

God Is Our Very Present Help

In my dark bedroom that morning, I wondered why He was so silent. But here's what was going on: God smiled while I pouted, painted while I complained, and then led me to a sunrise that forever left me changed.

We cannot live by what our eyes see and must not build a theology based on our experiences. If God's Word is our plumb line, our true north, and our compass, then our experiences will often reinforce what He's already said. But we must be careful not to think something is true simply because we've experienced it as so. Some of our experiences lie to us. Some of what we feel is from an accumulation of unresolved pain that significantly skews our perspective. Some of our thought processes need dismantling and rewiring.

Thankfully, this is not a process we're left to handle on our own. Nobody knows you and loves you like our Abba. He's merciful with your weakness and tender with your tears. He knows how to extract lies from your belief system while preserving your precious heart. He's quite aware of the Enemy's consistent and constant attempts to steal from you, and He intends to deal with His adversary and restore you. But He's not rushing you through your process. He's not in a hurry. He moves at the pace of grace. Healing is sometimes hard work. But God is "a *very present* help in trouble."[10]

My friend Carra recently shared this thought with me: "A lot of the journey can be very painful as He extricates the lies from you, resets bones and thought processes, and pours ointment in the wounds so they can heal. I wouldn't say I have enjoyed the healing journey in all its parts, but it has been *good*."

English poet Elizabeth Barrett Browning penned one of my favorite quotes of all time: "Earth's crammed with heaven, And every common bush afire with God; But only he who sees, takes off his shoes, The rest sit round it and pluck blackberries."[11]

God is everywhere. He's there with you in the morning when the sun peeks over the horizon, and He's there in the storm when you can't find your footing. He's there with the giggling kids at the corner lemonade stand, and He's there on the ICU floor, ready to welcome His child home.

His handiwork is everywhere too. We see His breathtaking display in each flower and in the daily gift of sunrises and sunsets. We behold His creative wonder in the sound of singing birds and in the fluttering wings of butterflies. Nobody can take credit for this artistry but God.

And He's especially taken with you. Chip Ingram wrote:

As a new creation in Christ, you become a new person. "The old things passed away; behold, new things have come" (2 Corinthians 5:17 NASB). The common illustration for this metamorphosis is one we learned in basic biology. A caterpillar creates a chrysalis, and out comes a butterfly. The little green caterpillar and the bright, beautiful butterfly have exactly the same DNA, but a fundamental transformation has taken place. The caterpillar has taken on a new nature. It has new capabilities. It is no longer small and ugly; it is beautiful and new.[12]

The heavens declare the glory of God,
the skies proclaim the work of his hands.
Day after day they pour forth speech,
night after night they reveal knowledge.
They have no speech, they use no words,
no sound is heard from them.
Yet their voice goes out into all the earth,
their words to the ends of the world.
In the heavens God has pitched a tent for the sun.
It is like a bridegroom coming out of his chamber,
like a champion rejoicing to run his course.
It rises at one end of the heavens
and makes its circuit to the other,
nothing is deprived of its warmth.

PSALM 19:1–6 (NIV)

May you—starting today—awaken to the wonder of God's brilliant presence. May the profound evidence of His handiwork bring life to your soul. May you slow down long enough to behold beauty, and may you take the time to appreciate His intelligent design. Whatever you know of God, know this—*there's more.*

We obviously don't worship nature; we worship God. But we magnify Him when we acknowledge the work of His hands. He is God and there is no one like Him.

May you develop a lifelong habit of response. Open your eyes, see the sky, and thank Jesus. Open your mouth, taste the rain, and worship God. Open your ears, hear the sounds of nature, and sing along. And then offer your whole life to Him—the One who created you. Out of all creation, you are one of His most remarkable works of art. You are a masterpiece.

Reflect

1. Though God passionately and consistently loves us, most of us only conditionally trust Him, if we're honest. We lose sight of His goodness when life's not good. We let go of His promises when they seem incongruent with our current reality. Yet He is more trustworthy than our circumstances. Circumstances change. God will always be good. Write about a time when you (like me) accused God of being someone He's not, and it turned out that you were wrong, not Him. How did God meet you in that circumstance? If you've never had such an experience, write about a time when you doubted that God was who He promised to be.

2. Read Romans 8:1–9. Pause on verse 6 and answer this question: As it pertains to God's presence and your awareness of His presence, how might the sinful nature Paul talked about here cause you to misinterpret your circumstances?

3. Still pondering verse 6, answer this second question: If you

allow the Holy Spirit to guide and guard your thoughts, Scripture says you'll have peace. Is it possible to walk through a time where God seems silent yet still enjoy a sense of His peace? Write down your thoughts.

4. Read Romans 8:31–39 and reflect on the juxtaposition of pain and presence. If nothing can separate us from His love, and He is love, then nothing can separate us from Him. And if you still wonder if that's true, read Psalm 139 and write out a personalized, paraphrased version of Romans 8:31–39, letting the psalm guide you. I'm praying faith awakens your heart as you write.

Pray

High King of Heaven, mighty and matchless God, I humbly bow before You. There is no God like You! I long to know You more, trust You more, and experience You more than before. Show me what lies I began believing when life let me down. Reveal to me the countless subtle ways the Enemy seeks to distract me from You. I want to be fiercely focused on You, Your will, and Your ways. Awaken my heart to know Your Word, trust Your voice, and believe what You say. Work wonders in and through me, Lord. May my life be an offering that glorifies You and nourishes many. In Jesus' name I pray, amen.

Respond

Worship God because He is who He is. Give thanks to Him for all He's done, for all you possess in Him. Speak to your soul if necessary, and tell yourself to trust in God once again. Remember, He's actively engaged in your story. He's singing over you, changing the atmosphere because of you, and excited about what He has planned for you. There's no law anywhere that says He needs to check in with you or run everything by you. He invites you to trust Him. Just wait until you see what He's been up to.

> Did you know that God is singing songs of deliverance all around you all the time? You can't hear them because they're outside your range of hearing, but you're surrounded by a sonic shield. Those songs of deliverance are powerful enough to break any bondage, overcome any addiction, and solve any problem. Those songs are the reason no weapon formed against you will prosper.[13]
>
> MARK BATTERSON

Ponder His Presence

What Does It Mean to Quench the Holy Spirit?

We were at the concert of a young, up-and-coming recording artist when he was still doing shows in high school gymnasiums. His lyrics reflected on God's faithfulness through the years. The lights were low, he gently played his guitar, and we sang along with reverent awe. We felt God's manifest presence settle upon the room. It was so tangible you could touch it. You could've heard a pin drop.

The artist, sensitive to the Holy Spirit, whispered a prayer, and we lingered in silence while he strummed a few chords. People opened their hands and whispered their own prayers. Some started to weep. It was a taste of heaven.

Suddenly, the mic squealed with feedback as the event host stepped in front of the artist and grabbed the mic from its stand. He tapped on the mic and then jarringly ended the moment by asking for an offering—because, you know, these kinds of events don't pay for themselves. I peeked at our worship leader as he dropped his head in sadness. If the Holy Spirit is a fire, then this event host doused the flame with a bucket of water.

First Thessalonians 5:19–21 says, "Do not quench the Spirit. Do not despise prophecies. Test all things; hold fast what is good" (NKJV). The word "quench" in this verse means to extinguish, douse, suppress, or stifle.[1] The study note in one of my Bibles reads, "Quenching may be either by an inadequate, chilled response, or an exaggerated, disruptive response."[2] One of the great griefs in the body of Christ is how some have neglected or even vilified the Holy Spirit. Why? Because others have taken the supernatural and made it sensational. They've moved from humble, reverent awe to celebrity-driven showmanship. God, forgive us.

To disassociate from such activity, some have moved to another and equally heartbreaking extreme. They view the Trinity this way: the Father, Son, and God's Holy Word. The Word of God is our plumb line, but the Holy Spirit is the third member of the Trinity. We miss out on so much when we push Him out of our gatherings to maintain control.

What are some ways that we can quench the Holy Spirit? Legalism quenches the Spirit. A love for control quenches the Spirit. The fear of man can quench the Spirit.

Hypersuspicion is not the same as holy discernment. If you've been jaded by misuses of power and out-of-control meetings to the point that you're suspicious of *any* heartfelt response to God, you may be at risk for quenching a genuine move of God.

You may feel more *comfortable* in a controlled setting, but what you may actually *need* is to experience God in a way that you cannot deny and cannot explain. God knows what you're afraid of, and He knows what aspect of His character you still need to understand. If you're willing to leave the familiar for the purpose of experiencing God in a fresh new way, He just might surprise you.

I believe we're coming into a day where God will move despite denominational preferences. He will make Himself known in ways that convict, empower, overwhelm, and affirm who He is. He'll make Himself known in ways we need to know Him so we can navigate the days ahead.

Prayer

Lord, forgive me for trusting my ability to keep order more than I trust Your ability to move mightily in my midst. Remove my jaded lens and give me a hunger to encounter You in a way that forever changes me.

three

God Is Good

Are You Ready to Trust Him?

I don't want to look back on my life—my beautiful, wonder-filled, God-given life—and realize that I've mostly missed it while I was busy preparing for the worst.

NICOLE ZASOWSKI

She approached my book table with a fierce gaze and a kind smile. She towered over me like a six-foot angel, but I knew she was a real person because she walked alongside a precious friend. Most of the conferees were on their way home. My husband, Kev, packed up our books after a fantastic event. Because I'm someone who's battled publicly (for a long time) with Lyme disease and mold toxicity, countless people have approached me to pray for me, give me advice, or encourage me to hang on and hang in there. All of it means so much to me. But this encounter was quite different from all the others.

39

Let's back up for a bit of context. My favorite holidays are Christmas and Easter. Yet each Easter holiday for the past seven years or more has been heartbreakingly disappointing. I inwardly hope for a miracle, believe for a miracle, pray for a miracle—*maybe this year will be different*—but I end up with a surge of symptoms that moves me to tears. Springtime must be a bad season for Lyme/mold symptoms.

Last year was the worst. The night before Easter, I walked the floor most of the night, trying to breathe deeply and pray Scripture. My heart kept beating erratically and pounding in my chest. Numbing surged from my neck up into my jaw. My ears rang at a feverish pitch. I felt so much pressure in my head it triggered TMJ spasms in my jaw. A cascade of inflammation surged through my body. I couldn't get away from myself. I didn't know what to do. So I went down into the basement, paced the floor, cried out to God, took deep breaths, and spoke the Word over my life, health, family, and church. By morning, I felt like I'd been hit by a truck.

My sister's family planned to join us for an Easter brunch. When they walked in the door, they saw me sitting at the counter with my face in my hands, crying like I'd never stop. My son Jake and his wife, Lizzie, also arrived. Because they're all just wonderful, beautiful people, they didn't miss a beat. Never mind the brunch; they surrounded me and started to pray. Each appealed to God for mercy, healing, and relief from these wretched symptoms. My nephew Noah came close, put his hand on my shoulder, and prayed, "Thank You, Lord. I believe You have a plan for Susie to cross over from a ministry of trial to a ministry of triumph."

A surge of a different kind shot through my body. I knew I'd just heard the Word of the Lord.

Weeks prior, during a particularly intense time of prayer, I had cried out to the Lord, "Show me what I'm missing, Lord! I feel like I'm army-crawling for inches. What am I not seeing?" He whispered back with great clarity, *You may be only gaining inches in the natural, but you're gaining miles in the spiritual realm.* I imagined myself running through a forest like a Navy SEAL (I like to imagine that I'm a SEAL), tacking right and left. I was behind enemy lines, but I was running with agility and endurance. Suddenly, I came to an opening in the trees and saw a raging river, but I didn't slow down. I took a leap of faith, and all at once an unseen hand propelled me across the river. When I landed, I bounded forward with newfound power and strength in every step.

Hope fluttered within me. A time of "crossing over" was up ahead for me. I just knew it. So when Noah prayed his prayer about crossing over, I felt my soul quiver with life.

I did my best to stay expectant, hopeful, and joyful for the rest of the year. I had good days and a lot of bad days. But deep inside, I knew God was moving on my behalf, and soon I would see it.

Author and pastor Craig Groeschel said something the last time he was on my show, and it keeps replaying in my thoughts: "When it's not God's time, you can't force it. When it is God's time, you can't stop it."

> "When it's not God's time, you can't force it. When it is God's time, you can't stop it."
>
> CRAIG GROESCHEL

Surprised by God's Presence

Though I continued onward with a sense of holy expectancy, I didn't anticipate what would happen this past Lenten season. God rarely shows up in the ways we expect Him to, and He caught me by complete surprise this time. Over several days, three unrelated groups of women approached me with a confident boldness and said, "The Lord has charged us to pray for you until you are healed." I'll weave more of this story throughout the book because it forever changed me. But suffice to say, God's goodness chased after me when He mobilized women to approach me with an assignment *to see me healed*. I've battled for thirty-two years. Could this be God's time for me?

One of those women is Maria—the six-foot-tall angel who's really a human. She leaned over the table so we could see eye to eye. With a beautiful blend of humility, boldness, confidence, and conviction, she whispered to me, "Susie, I sense the Lord wants you to know that He's proud of you. He's seen how hard you've fought to stand in faith while battling this long-term illness. You need to know that you're not standing here unhealed because you lack faith. Your fight has not been wasted on you. You've gained so much over the years and helped many people find courage in their own battles. And when God heals you, He will propel you forward and use you to help many others cross over to a place of healing, wholeness, and abundance. My husband and I have a prayer ministry, and we'd consider it a great honor to stand with you and pray with you so that you can walk free."

Maria's words affirmed the things God had been saying to me. I was exhausted from the battle, but, at that moment, expectancy stirred within me.

Amazingly, God would have it that I'd meet with these three separate groups of women just days apart from each other. It was like a one-two-three punch against this affliction that had plagued me for so long. Thus began a new phase in my miracle healing journey.

In the days and weeks that followed, Maria and I audio-texted back and forth. I'd tell her if I had a rough day of symptoms, and she'd pray over the phone with me. When Maria sent me audio texts, I'd get out my notepad and take notes. One thing she pounded home to me until it seeped into my heart, mind, and cells was this: "Surely only goodness and mercy follow you! *Surely*, they do! If you're not living with a holy expectancy that God is up to something good, even when life is hard—especially when life is hard—then something is out of alignment within you. Your core beliefs need to be based on God's Word, not your experiences. God is only and always good. You can trust Him. He wants to heal your hurts, uproot the lies, and shut down the inroads where the Enemy has had repeated access to steal from you. A day is coming where you will live with joyful, giddy expectancy over all the good God is up to in your life."

Though I'd certainly been on the receiving end of so much of God's goodness, much of it was lost on me because I didn't feel well most days. Though I enjoyed great moments of worship, prayer, and time in the Word; though I loved spending time with family and friends and experienced gratitude for the work God had assigned to me; my inner self constantly braced for impact, waiting for the next surge to knock me over. Like I was looking at my life through plexiglass—I could see it, but I couldn't really taste it, touch it, or enjoy it like I longed to.

A Lifestyle of Holy Expectancy

It's natural to develop habits and certain beliefs around our experiences. When we get knocked around enough by life, without even thinking about it, we may subtly shift our expectancy away from God and onto our own ability to protect and deliver ourselves. It's a natural response to life on a fallen planet, but it leaves us exhausted and disillusioned, with our eyes downward instead of upward.

I've talked about and taught the importance of renewing our minds and framing our trials with a faith perspective. But I didn't realize that a renewed mind and a faith perspective will only take you as far as your capacity to know and believe that God really is good. It's supernatural to cultivate a lifestyle of holy expectancy despite circumstances we've experienced and hardships we've endured.

> A renewed mind and a faith perspective will only take you as far as your capacity to know and believe that God really is good.

During a long stretch of hard days, I prayed the Word back to God: "Lord, my hope has been deferred for so long that my heart feels sick. I'm trying to keep the faith, but I'm weary in the battle." I suddenly felt convicted. Was this misplaced lament? I sensed the nudge to look deeper into that verse to ensure I wasn't taking it out of context.

Proverbs 13:12 says, "Hope deferred makes the heart sick, but a dream fulfilled is a tree of life." Imagine my surprise when I realized that the word "deferred" in this verse is a verb. It's an action word. I wasn't heartsick over the delayed answers to my prayers. I was heartsick because *I'd deferred* my hope. I had put it aside because I was tired of waiting for a breakthrough.

Based on God's Word, we have every reason for and provision to access love, joy, peace, patience, kindness, goodness, faithfulness, gentleness, and self-control,[1] no matter the season of life. Why? Because we abide in the Vine,[2] the source of life and Christlike virtue.

God's life-giving fruit is not reserved for trouble-free times; it's a testament to God's miracle mightily at work within us despite the times. I'd forgotten who I was and lost sight of who God was. Exactly and always, the Enemy's aim against us is to make us forget who we are and dim our view of God's miraculous and marvelous goodness. I had set aside hope for another day. It's no wonder I was exhausted. Here's what I learned: putting off hope postpones courage and makes the heart sick

Our hearts can't live without hope and courage! You can't simultaneously trust God and think destructive thoughts. You can't at once brace for impact and draw near to God with a sense of expectancy. We *choose* to trust God. But trusting Him is difficult when the message of our circumstances upstages the life-changing message of His goodness.

A Power Like No Other

For months during a particularly long stretch of difficult days, God kept me reciting a passage from the book of Jeremiah:

> Thus says the LORD:
> "Cursed is the man who trusts in man
> And makes flesh his strength,

Whose heart departs from the LORD.
For he shall be like a shrub in the desert,
And shall not see when good comes,
But shall inhabit the parched places in the wilderness,
In a salt land which is not inhabited."[3]

Here is my paraphrase of this passage:

She who trusts in herself
Or puts her hope in human strength
Or in man-made systems
She who refuses to trust God with her story
Will stunt her own growth
She'll not see good when it comes
She'll miss the new sprouts of fresh life all around her
Because her eyes are on her barren field
She'll decide that God's not good
And she'll be wrong.

The next verses in the book of Jeremiah go on to say:

But blessed are those who trust in the LORD
and have made the LORD their hope and confidence.[4]
They are like trees planted along a riverbank,
with roots that reach deep into the water.
Such trees are not bothered by the heat
or worried by long months of drought.
Their leaves stay green,
and they never stop producing fruit.[5]

Here is my paraphrase of this passage:

She who trusts God to be marvelous because He's God
finds Him faithful beyond her wildest dreams
She's no longer intimidated by uncertainty
She knows and believes that goodness is on its way
She holds unswervingly to hope
because she's fiercely confident that God is faithful
She bears nourishing fruit in season and bursts
     with life throughout her days
God is a life force for everyone who counts on Him
for strength, deliverance, and breakthrough.

We're tethered to a good Father. A majestic Savior. A power like no other. He's not moody, grumpy, or inconsistent. He is, however, fiercely protective, full of justice, and completely unpredictable. Yet everything He does aligns with His goodness and faithfulness.

When God Seems Unkind

Once upon a time, a particular city was on friendly terms with Israel. But over time it grew more wicked in its ways, greedy in its actions, and ungodly in its views toward God's people. A mom and her daughter lived in that city. The mom was brokenhearted because her daughter was tormented by evil spirits. I shudder to imagine the trauma this little one endured at the hands of the Enemy and his minions.

Scripture doesn't give us the names of this mother and daughter, so let's call this woman Ariel and her little girl Bella. This is how I imagine the scene in Matthew 15:21–28: Ariel had heard rumors about a man of compassion who healed the sick and delivered the oppressed. And He'd come to town! Driven by her deep love for little Bella, Ariel frantically left her simple home and wove through the crowd, determined to find answers. Whenever she saw a familiar face, she grabbed fistfuls of their sleeves, pulled them close, and asked, "Tell me, do you know where He is? The Healer! Where is He staying?"

She didn't stop to formulate a plan or consider the possible outcome for a woman who dared to barge unannounced into a gathering of men. For Bella's sake, Ariel determined to act now and deal with the consequences later. She bravely entered the home of strangers, then crumpled into a heap at the feet of Jesus. She grabbed hold of His ankles and cried out, "Please, sir! Help my baby! She's tormented by an evil spirit. I've tried to help her, but she's captive. She's my little girl. Please help her!"

Throughout the Gospels, we see that Jesus' compassion compelled Him to action. But it was His wisdom that caused Him to delay. As I read the Gospel account of this woman, I was cheering for Ariel. I wanted Jesus to grab her hands, look her in the eyes, vindicate her faith, and speak life into little Bella at that very moment. But Jesus—always keeping the bigger picture in mind—had other plans. Since Ariel was a Gentile, born in Syrian Phoenicia (part of the Roman Empire), Jesus told her, in essence, "First I should feed the children—My own family, the Jews. It isn't right to take food from children and throw it to the dogs."

Ouch. But there's more to this story. First, we see there is an order to the things of God. He has a purpose in His processes. Our story, our desperate needs, are never all about us. God answers our prayers when He'll get the most glory and can reach the most significant number of people with our story. God is on a global rescue mission. He delights in every detail of your life. But He also knows who needs to hear your story and see your life before and after your breakthrough.

> **God answers our prayers when He'll get the most glory and can reach the most significant number of people with our story.**

Yet sometimes God makes exceptions to His own rules. For example, Jesus turned water into wine when His "time [had] not yet come."[6] Why? Because Mary was His mother. And she had such fierce faith that even when Jesus told her it was too early for miracles, she turned to the servants and said, "Do whatever he tells you."[7] I love that moment in Scripture.

The prophecies foretold that the Messiah would come to God's chosen people. But there were hints in the Old Testament that this message of salvation would also—in due time—be available to Gentiles.[8] Thankfully, the gospel opened to Gentiles and the whole world; otherwise most of us would be without hope! Even so, Jesus could have spoken in a kinder tone to Ariel, no? But who's to say He didn't look at Ariel with kindness in His eyes? Maybe He even cracked a smile, opened His hands, and invited her to dialogue with Him. Whatever Jesus did at that moment, His posture invited Ariel to move toward Him, not away from Him. She dared to engage with Jesus and lay hold of the promise He had for her.

On the surface, Jesus' words may seem harsh and unsympathetic, but the woman recognized them as a wide-open door to God's throne. Jesus did not use the negative term for "dogs" that referred to scavengers (the word sometimes used by Jews to refer to Gentiles); instead, he used the term for a household pet. The woman took the cue and added to his analogy of pets under a family dining table. *Her attitude was expectant and hopeful, not prickly or hypersensitive.* She knew what she wanted, and she believed Jesus could provide. *We could learn from this woman's singular purpose and optimistic resilience.* Jesus really does want to meet our needs. When we pray, we're talking to a friend.[9]

Years ago, I spoke with John Eldredge about the Syrophoenician woman, and he suggested that Jesus' words to her were more for the disciples than for her. Jesus intended to answer the woman's plea, but He also wanted to teach His followers an important lesson. Eldredge thinks Jesus knew the Syrophoenician woman had a feisty faith and could handle the banter of their exchange and that His purpose for the seemingly harsh words were to challenge His disciples' prejudices.

Somehow, Ariel discerned an opening, an opportunity to challenge the status quo and lay hold of the miracle she desperately needed. When Jesus told Ariel He needed to feed His own family first, she quickly replied, "That's true, Lord. But even the dogs under the table are allowed to eat the scraps from the children's plates." Jesus was so moved by her humble persistence that He granted her request. I imagine that moment when Jesus opened His hands, smiled, and said, "Great answer! Go home to your little girl. The demon has left her." I picture tears escaping Ariel's eyes as she covered her face with her hands. Her cheeks flushed at the thought of the miracle her family had just experienced. She headed out the door, turned one last time, thanked

Jesus for His kindness, and ran home without stopping. She entered her home breathless, only to find sweet Bella resting and at peace. Sometimes faith compels us to step outside the cultural norms to experience God.

Wouldn't you say the same about the woman with the issue of blood that we read about in the Gospels?[10] People expected her to stay home and live in isolation. Yet she had tried that, and it only made things worse. She stepped out of her small story, pressed through the crowds, grabbed hold of Jesus' hem, and her life was forever changed. We're still talking about her today.

> **Prayer is not the overcoming of God's reluctance but the laying hold of God's willingness.**[11]
> MARTIN LUTHER

Don't Miss His Goodness!

Let's revisit the previous passage from Jeremiah. Is it possible to miss goodness when it comes? There will be times when we're still waiting to see His goodness manifest in a particular area of our lives. This is when we're tempted to seek out our own solutions and preempt our own outcomes. Our strivings may help us gain ground in the short term but always prove disappointing and sometimes even disastrous in the end.

Proverbs 19:3 says, "People ruin their lives by their own foolishness and then are angry at the LORD." It's tempting to connect the painful dots in our story and draw a wrong conclusion about ourselves and God. And that's what the Enemy wants from us.

Because if we keep at the forefront of our minds all the hardships we've faced, we'll live instinctively bracing for impact.

Waiting for the other shoe to drop is terrible for our health, brain, and spiritual life. And it's in direct conflict with the promises of God. Search the Scriptures for verses about God's goodness, and you'll find they're often connected to the invitation to trust, wait, and believe.

At some point, we need to trust God to be good. It's a vulnerable leap, I know. Moreover, sometimes we're called to move past static trust and boldly decide to wrestle with God. Not because He's withholding a blessing but because we've got to wrestle through our reluctance to trust Him. Every one of our not-yet seasons reveals our buried beliefs about God and ourselves. And our opinions about both often change with the season.

God knows what's in us, but He wants *us* to know what's in us so we'll learn to trust Him. Perhaps the more we trust Him, the more we'll experience His presence and begin to truly believe that He is good. And the more we trust His goodness, the greater our story becomes. Not only for us but for the many who are desperate to know that the One who put the stars in place is ultimately working all things together for the good of those who love Him and are called according to His purpose.

Meanwhile, the moment we get tired in the waiting, God's Spirit is right alongside helping us along. If we don't know how or what to pray, it doesn't matter.

He does our praying in and for us, making prayer out of our wordless sighs, our aching groans. He knows us far better than we know ourselves, knows our pregnant condition, and keeps us present before God. That's why we can be so sure that every detail in our lives of love for God is worked into something good.

ROMANS 8:26–28 (MSG)

Reflect

1. Consider the boldness of some of the women mentioned in Scripture:[12] Ruth, Esther, Deborah, Mary the mother of Jesus, the Samaritan woman, the woman with the issue of blood, and the Syrophoenician woman (whom I called "Ariel"). These women were not content to take a passive role in their stories. Once they saw themselves in the bigger story, they acted, and God moved. Where are you right now with regard to your posture of expectancy? Bracing for impact—static faith—or wrestling with God? Explain.

2. Pick one of the women mentioned above, read her story in Scripture, and explain why you chose her. Then answer the following question: At what point in her story did she decide to act? Explain.

3. Even though God isn't always mentioned in every story, He's involved. Where do you see His involvement in the story you read?
4. How does her story tie to your story?

Pray

Dear precious Father, forgive me for the countless times I've looked to my circumstances more than Your Word to determine what I think about You. When I read Scripture, I learn that You are good, kind, and trustworthy. And that's why my faith matters so much to You. Help me to learn to trust You. Remind me of the countless ways You've come through for me in the past. I have a history with You, and I have a future too. Show me who's watching my life so I remember that my story is a part of a much bigger story than I can see right now. I can never get away from Your presence, which means I can never get away from Your goodness. Help me develop a healthy, holy expectancy. I want to joyfully and continually look for Your goodness. I've spent enough time rehearsing my fears. I'm done bracing for impact. It's time for me to rehearse Your promises. Help me to trust You more with each passing day. Amen.

Respond

Refrain from making negative assessments and statements about yourself, God, and your circumstances. Instead, train your eyes and thoughts to actively look for God's movement in your life. Immerse yourself in passages that speak of God's strength, power, goodness, and kindness. In a particularly tough season, this discipline will serve you incredibly well. God asks that we suspend judgment in the short term and dare to believe that He's kinder than we ever imagined and more purposeful with our story than we can possibly fathom. Remember the story about our girl Ariel? She wasn't hypersensitive or prickly. She possessed singular focus and optimistic resilience. May we set our faces like flint on the One who knows us, loves us, and is moving heaven and earth on our behalf. May we be optimistically resilient.

Ponder His Presence

How Do I Know If I'm Hearing the Voice of God?

Religious leaders gathered around Jesus and demanded a sign—proof that He indeed was the Messiah. Picture them mumbling under their breath, glaring through slitted eyes, and waiting for Jesus to make a wrong move. Jesus wasn't fooled for a second. Here's how He replied:

> "I have already told you, and you don't believe me. The proof is the work I do in my Father's name. But you don't believe me because you are not my sheep. My sheep listen to my voice; I know them, and they follow me. I give them eternal life, and they will never perish. No one can snatch them away from me, for my Father has given them to me, and he is more powerful than anyone else. No one can snatch them from the Father's hand. The Father and I are one."[1]

It's the pure in heart who see God.[2] Those bent on accusing

Jesus couldn't see Him for who He was. But if we are in Christ, Christ is in us. He opens the eyes of our hearts. He imparts divine wisdom to us and tells us things we'd otherwise never know or comprehend. He loves us with an everlasting love. No one can snatch us out of His hand.

He speaks to us in a variety of ways: sometimes through His Word, or a song, or a friend, or a simple impression in your heart. Sometimes wisdom enters your heart and His knowledge fills you with joy.[3] If you love Jesus, spend time in His Word and seek to obey Him in all your ways. You can trust that God is leading you (even when you're unaware). He'll never waver in His commitment to you.

We complicate things when we expect God to talk to us the way He talks to others. Or we see someone who claims to hear Him in detail and we wonder why we don't enjoy such clarity. But if we can learn to trust His love and enjoy His presence, we'll eventually learn to rest in His care. We'll go about our day, trusting that if we're about to lose our way, the Holy Spirit will convict and correct us as needed. And if there's something we need to know, God will make sure to let us know.

Oswald Chambers wrote these wise words about hearing the voice of God:

The voice of the Spirit of God is as gentle as a summer breeze—so gentle that unless you are living in complete fellowship and oneness with God, you will never hear it. The sense of warning and restraint that the Spirit gives comes to us in the most amazingly gentle ways. And if you are not sensitive enough to detect His voice, you will quench it, and your spiritual life will be impaired. This sense of restraint will always come as a "still small voice" (1 Kings 19:12), so faint that no one except a saint of God will notice it.[4]

Prayer

Dear Jesus, You know me and I know You. Help me to trust in Your love, listen for Your voice, and respond when You speak. I want to hear from You. You want to speak to me. My soul waits for You. Amen.

four

God Is Awesome

Take Off Your Shoes

When we see Jesus as Commander of the army of the Lord, [it is our job] to fall on our faces before Him and worship—that is, to confess the self-will, self-effort, and self-glory that have dominated us and deeply surrender to Him as our Commander, and be willing for Him to make the decisions, give the orders, and be the doer of the work. . . . We cannot be too low at His feet if He is to cause the walls of our Jericho to fall. He will have no difficulty with those walls if He can get us to fall first.

ROY HESSION

During my college years, I didn't have a lot of spiritual support on my faith journey. I wandered into the ways of the world and then back toward the heart of God again. One morning in my dorm room, I repented and cried out to God. I spent time in His Word and sensed His great love for me. Joy returned to my soul. I went to class unaware of what God was about to do that day. For starters, I met a couple of classmates—identical twins. Dark hair. Bright countenances. And such sweet dispositions. I noticed they kept looking my way during class. I smiled, gave them a nod, and returned my attention to our instructor.

Right in the middle of the lecture, one of the sisters leaned over and said, "There's something different about you. You have so much joy. Will you tell us why you have joy?"

I whispered back, "I'd love to talk with you more. Let's meet after class." I followed these girls to their dorm room and told them about Jesus. Their hearts were so tender and receptive that they were instantly in awe of God. One of them got up abruptly and said, "Be right back!"

Within minutes, she grabbed a few friends and dragged them back into our conversation. I introduced my new friends to Jesus, and they wholeheartedly accepted Him. Over the next few weeks we hosted more gatherings with the girls on their dorm floor. They asked questions, and I did my best to answer them. Their hunger for God activated a faith that I'd almost neglected.

One day while crammed in a van with a bunch of other college students on our way home for the weekend, I curled up with a book by Watchman Nee. I don't recall the title, but I do remember what happened. I went from being half involved with the surrounding conversations and partially attuned to what I was reading to suddenly focusing on the words on the page. At that moment I had an encounter with God unlike anything I'd ever experienced up to that point. His Spirit drew near, and I could not hide from Him. Like a movie reel, I saw my life's story unwind before me. I saw my life in fast motion, one deed after another, and the motivations that fueled my actions.

A consistent theme ran throughout my life. Everything I'd done—good, bad, and otherwise—was to rescue my sense of self-worth. Most of my good deeds were to prove myself. Most sinful indulgences were to escape from myself. Though God can and did redeem every aspect of my story, all my strivings were wasted efforts.

I'd misused my time, treasure, and talents to prove something that Jesus had already done, had already won. I didn't know any better then. But I did now. In that van I came face-to-face with the truth about my depravity and the power of God's holy standard for me. There'd be no dabbling in this walk of faith. God was not one to be trifled with. He wasn't messing around. I couldn't escape Him.

I gasped. I trembled. I covered my mouth with my hands, and tears escaped my eyes.

Friends asked if I was okay, and I could only shake my head. I couldn't speak. I dared not justify my ways. I was guilty of selfish, self-preserving efforts. Though I had reason to be painfully insecure, I learned that insecurity is just another form of selfishness. Self-preservation and kingdom life are entirely incompatible.

To live out of a lie is to perpetuate more lies. God had drawn near. I felt no condemnation, but I was absolutely undone with conviction. To place the reel of my life up against the backdrop of God's majesty and holiness left me breathless. I was a believer at this point, yet for some reason I was still trying to save myself. I didn't understand the potent power of the gospel. My efforts were worthless. My God was holy. If I could have gone facedown in the van, I would have. For the next three days I barely said a word. I didn't want to interrupt the cleansing fire of the Holy Spirit at work in me.

Looking back over the years that I've followed the Messiah, I can now see how intimately He's been involved in my life. Even during those seasons when God seemed silent and life was just a daily grind, Jesus led, interceded, guarded, and guided my way—all while I was unaware.

He put the right people in my path at just the right time. He prompted me to turn right when I would have turned left. He nudged me to make a phone call when I was headed for the ditch of despair. He introduced a new friend when I needed a fresh perspective. He played a song that inspired faith in the middle of my doubts. He put dreams in my heart and dared me to agree with Him. He gave me insight into intercession and invited me to join Him. He gave me opportunities to forgive, trust, and release my cares to Him, knowing how these processes would transform me and tether my heart to His.

> Ever and always, God allows enough challenges to keep us dependent, enough goodness to keep us encouraged, and enough grace to sustain us.

Ever and always, God allows enough challenges to keep us dependent, enough goodness to keep us encouraged, and enough grace to sustain us.

Though I lived through plenty of seasons with a broken heart, wishing things were different than they were, I never lacked any of what I needed. God has always been faithful, always guided, always provided. Life on earth is hard. But we serve an awesome God.

I don't want to miss Him because I can't always sense His

nearness. Our lives burst with evidence that God is at work in our story. He charged the Israelites not to forget about His faithfulness. When we forget, we wander. When we recall and rehearse God's faithfulness in the past, we more clearly discern His goodness in the present.

Remembering is stewardship. Recalling is wisdom. Rehearsing is nourishment for our souls.

> When we forget, we wander. When we recall and rehearse God's faithfulness in the past, we more clearly discern His goodness in the present.

And I said, "This is my fate;
the Most High has turned his hand against me."
But then I recall all you have done, O LORD;
I remember your wonderful deeds of long ago.
They are constantly in my thoughts.
I cannot stop thinking about your mighty works.
O God, your ways are holy.
Is there any god as mighty as you?
You are the God of great wonders!
You demonstrate your awesome power among the
nations.[1]

It's good for our hearts to go back and recall the times when God invaded our everyday existence with tangible expressions of His love and power. Times when He allowed us a peek into the eternal realm in a way that totally shifted our perspective and deepened our assurance that God was near, God cared, and God was moving in our midst.

*We are all messed up like
a person compromised
with impurity,
even all our right efforts
are like soiled rags.
We're drying up like a leaf
in autumn and are blown
away by wrongdoing.*

ISAIAH 64:6 (The Voice)

Such moments in my life have left me speechless with awe and wonder. After walking with God for decades, I know this to be true: He's more present than I can comprehend and more powerful than I ever imagined.

Spending time this morning pondering my history with God reminds me that my present bursts with His power and my future is bright with hope. I've written about a number of these instances in other books, but I'm going to synopsize them here for context. I encourage you to take a trip down memory lane as well. It'll do wonders for your soul.

A Moment in My History with God

Another moment in my history that I'll not soon forget happened in the middle of the night. I was thick in the battle with Lyme disease. Our finances were upside down because of our medical debt. Our house was falling apart. And our cupboards were almost empty. Sickness raged through my body, and I felt pretty sure God had lost my address. Every night I begged God to intervene, yet it seemed my words never made it past our speckled-plaster ceiling. I even prayed, "If not for me, Lord, will you heal me for my children's sake? They need their mommy!"

I'd prayed, begged, whined, and complained. I felt sorry for myself and angry with God. But this night shook me to my core. God broke His silence. His presence drew near, and I was once again undone. He asked me with great clarity, *If I healed you, would you praise Me?* I said out loud, "Until the cows come home! I'll praise you all day and all night!"

Silence. I waited. Then His voice thundered in my heart: *Why is that? Will you praise Me because I am the Most High God and I gave My one and only Son for you? Or simply because you got your way?*

In the same way I'd experienced in college, God's holiness overshadowed my lowliness. It didn't matter that God wasn't giving me what I wanted. The bigger question was whether I was giving Him the glory He deserved.

I rolled out of bed and onto the floor. If I remember right, I tore my shirt in repentance. I do know I rent my heart. I was cut to the core. And this poem spilled out of me in the middle of the night.

A Time for Everything

I've walked through many storms
My prayers were filled with tears
The enemy was so big
Confirming all my fears
To a distant God
I would ever cry
Just wanting an answer
Always asking why

Yet heard I not from Him
Nor His angels singing
'Twas all that I could do
His robe to keep on clinging
Then suddenly, one night
As I beckoned Him to be
So real that I could feel Him
He finally spoke to me
Said He, "My daughter Susie
I love you with My life
No more would I e'er hurt you
Than be the cause of your strife
You see, it's not My hand
That's delivered all this pain
But it's true. My hand is there
To hold yours in the rain
It's something, how I'm good
To those whose life seems fair
And to those whose life is hard
'I never hear their prayer.'
It's something, how men see me
According to their need
Instead of faith and praise
They ask and beg and plead
I am a God who doesn't change with time
Nor change I with the season
I don't have to explain myself
Nor give you detailed reason
I've given all that I could give
When I gave to you My Son

I emptied out Myself for you
As if you were the only one
What I do, I do for you
Because I love you so
What I allow, I allow for you
Because I want you to grow
It's in faith, praise, and trust
You will find you are strong
When demands are replaced
With a faith-filled praise song
It is there you'll find peace
Where there once was strife
And it'll be just enough
To have Me in your life."

Shaken to the core, I realized that my relationship with God had been chiefly about what He could do for me. Yet if I kept God in my small story, I'd never mature and experience the riches of His love for all of humanity. I'd never step into the more remarkable story God was writing on the earth in my day.

I repented from the depths of my soul. I told the Lord that if He never healed me—although I'd hate it with all my heart—I would still praise Him. Going forward, I would follow Him on His terms, not mine. Until that night I knew Him as Savior, but at that moment He became my Lord.

God's presence changes everything. He didn't humiliate me. He humbled me. He didn't condemn me. He convicted me. He didn't shame me. He invited me to glorify Him in my sufferings, knowing how that process would utterly transform me and give the Enemy less real estate in my life.

Since we have been acquitted and made right through faith, we are able to experience true and lasting peace with God through our Lord Jesus, the Anointed One, the Liberating King. Jesus leads us into a place of radical grace where we are able to celebrate the hope of experiencing God's glory. And that's not all. We also celebrate in seasons of suffering because we know that when we suffer we develop endurance, which shapes our characters. When our characters are refined, we learn what it means to hope and anticipate God's goodness. And hope will never fail to satisfy our deepest need because the Holy Spirit that was given to us has flooded our hearts with God's love.

ROMANS 5:1–5 (THE VOICE)

Now I'm sure of this: the sufferings we endure now are not even worth comparing to the glory that is coming and will be revealed in us.

ROMANS 8:18 (THE VOICE)

The fire of my trials purified my heart and fortified my faith, allowing me to experience God in ways I had never dreamed possible. I know God. I know His Word. I'm aware of the Enemy's tactics. I know not to attempt this journey alone. I know to call prayer warriors when I'm in over my head. I know God inhabits the praises of His people.

I know things I didn't realize before my trials and before God charged me to follow Him on His terms, not mine. I think the same is true for you.

God-with-us. Emmanuel. An ever-present help in times of trouble. Our fortress. Strong tower. Shelter in the storm. Deliverer. Defender. Healer. Savior. Friend. Ponder this reality: the most powerful force in the universe cares deeply about your story.

What a wonderful God we serve!

A Fresh God-Encounter

Though I have several more stories like this, I'll share just one more.

I had a terrible cold. And my hip was out of joint. My nose was red. I walked with a limp. The only thing I was missing was a big hump on my back. I had a speaking event and felt strongly I needed to move ahead and fulfill my commitment. I was scheduled to speak six times in two days. I sat in the front row, waiting for the host to introduce me. It took all my strength not to lie down, curl up in a ball, and fall asleep.

My strength waned by the moment. But when it came time to step up and speak, I had energy in my body, power in my words, and clarity with my message. I spoke on prayer six times in two days. In between each message, I shriveled with exhaustion. And each time I stood up to speak, I experienced a supercharge of energy, clarity, and focus.

I didn't talk about healing (and didn't know much about it at that time in my life), yet several women were miraculously healed during my message. One shared how their sinus infection disappeared. Another shared how her back pain suddenly dissolved. In a moment, she was pain-free and felt great. The air was thick with a tangible sense of God's presence. Not from anything *I'd* done. God met them in that sanctuary.

It wasn't just the strength-when-I-needed-it miracle that stunned me. It was more the thick, tangible sense of God's presence and wonder in our midst. Women entered chattering and at once stopped talking. There was an expectancy in the room. A reverence that compelled us to silence.

I drove away from that event desperate to experience God like that again. I whispered, "What was that, God? And how can I have more of what I just experienced?" I crawled into bed, begged God to show me more of who He is, and then fell fast asleep. I had a vivid dream, which was totally unusual for me back then.

In my dream I saw beautiful, colorful clouds hovering just over people's heads. Lightning shot through and lit up the clouds.

Hues of smoky gray, deep purple, and bright whites were soaked with the presence and power of God. Just below, people went about their everyday lives, completely unaware of the power available to them. Occasionally someone would reach up and grab a handful of the power and put it on their heart or their child's head. But then, in the dream, I noticed one woman who camped in the presence. She reached up continually, grabbed handfuls of power, and placed them on herself, her children, and many of the strangers who passed by. Then I woke up. I was still sick—but truly in awe. I whispered, "Lord?" He replied, *Susie, most of My children scratch the surface of what I've made available to them.*

That experience forever changed my prayer life.

Burning Bushes and Holy Moments

Moses—once a prince of Egypt—ran for his life after taking the life of another. He landed in Midian and married the daughter of a priest. Given the family he'd married into, he likely engaged in faith conversations on occasion. But talking *about God* and encountering *the presence of God* are two distinctly different things. One day while tending the flocks, he came upon Mount Sinai, known as the mountain of God.

Moses noticed a flaming bush that burned without being consumed. He drew closer out of curiosity. Imagine the scene. Moses, gritty and grimy from working the land. Having spent years in obscurity, with little sense of vision or direction for his life, he stumbles upon a flaming bush while tending his flocks. What may seem happenstance to Moses is a divine circumstance orchestrated by God.

Imagine the brilliance of the orange-yellow glow flaming like a torch in the wilderness. The burning bush warms his face and makes his skin tingle. Yet the fire doesn't dwindle, and not an inch of the bush is consumed. He looks around to see if he's alone. Jarred back to the scene in front of him, Moses stumbles backward as God's voice thunders from the middle of the bush. *Moses! Moses!*

A burning bush in the middle of the desert. A thundering voice. And it's speaking the name of Moses.

> When the LORD saw Moses coming to take a closer look, God called to him from the middle of the bush, "Moses! Moses!"
>
> "Here I am!" Moses replied.
>
> "Do not come any closer," the LORD warned. "Take off your sandals, for you are standing on holy ground. I am the God of your father—the God of Abraham, the God of Isaac, and the God of Jacob." When Moses heard this, he covered his face because he was afraid to look at God.[2]

When God Breaks Through

We go about our days; we serve, give, live; we endure dry seasons where God seems silent. We do our best and trust God with the rest.

But none of that prepares us for those moments when God breaks through our earthbound perspective to make Himself known. We suddenly realize that He's so much more holy than we fathomed and more powerful than we imagined. Those moments remind us that we don't have the control we once thought. We don't have any power in and of ourselves. We don't know what we don't know.

Whenever the Almighty moves in and reveals His holy nature to us, we have a decision to make. Will we humble ourselves? Take off our shoes? Go facedown? Change direction? Seek to know Him more? Or will we explain away the experience, defaulting to our limited perspective and what's comfortable? Will we cover our ears and make some noise? Or will we cover our mouths and reverently listen?

God sometimes overwhelms us with His manifest presence because we're due for an upgrade in our perspective of who He is. God reveals His nature so that we might grow more confident in Him. We're securely tethered to the most immovable, unshakable force in the universe. If we grasped this truth in our inmost being, we'd likely never have another insecure day in our lives.

> God reveals His nature so that we might grow more confident in Him. We're securely tethered to the most immovable, unshakable force in the universe. If we grasped this truth in our inmost being, we'd likely never have another insecure day in our lives.

A.W. Tozer wrote, "It is impossible to keep our moral practices sound and our inward attitudes right while our idea of God is erroneous or inadequate. If we would bring back spiritual power to our lives, we must begin to think of God more nearly as He is."[3]

Whenever we see God manifest His power in Scripture, it reminds us that He alone is God. He is uncreated, has no limits, and has no rival. God exists outside of our timeframes and puny perspectives. He was, and is, and is to come. "'I am the Alpha and the Omega—the beginning and the end,' says the Lord God. 'I am the one who is, who always was, and who is still to come—the Almighty One.'"[4]

Rest assured that if you need an upgrade in your view of who God is, He'll meet you on the everyday path of life.

He moves in closer toward those who earnestly seek after Him. He may just whisper a truth your soul needs to hear. Or He may awaken you in the night with a prompt to pray. Or you may feel a conviction down into your bones when He rights your wrong thinking. The Lord God Almighty is in your midst. He's your fortress, your stronghold, and your deliverer. He understands that your experiences have skewed your perspective of Him. God longs for you to know Him the way He knows and loves you.

Beloved, now we are children of God, and it has not yet been revealed what we shall be, but we know that when He is revealed, we shall be like Him, for we shall see Him as He is.

1 JOHN 3:2 (NKJV)

Reflect

1. Moses first encountered God near Mount Sinai when he noticed a flaming bush. He drew near and the Lord spoke, changing the trajectory of Moses' life and the greater kingdom story. In Exodus 19, we find Moses back at Mount Sinai. Read Exodus 19 and write everything you observe about God's presence in this passage.

2. After Moses received the Ten Commandments, he came down from the mountain. Read Exodus 34:29–35 and note how God's glory rested on Moses. Write down your thoughts.

3. Read Psalm 34 and write about what most stands out to you in this passage. Ponder verse 5 and write out a personalized prayer around this verse.

4. Read 1 Kings 19:1–13 and imagine Elijah's state of mind. Consider a time when you felt battered by your storm and it seemed that the Enemy was winning the day. God met Elijah in this place. Picture Elijah conversing with God, who told him to stand on the mountain while the presence passed him. Wouldn't you imagine it was God when the wind started to blow? And when the earth began to shake—that must be God, right? But God wasn't in the wind or the earthquake. He manifested His presence after the shaking through a still, small voice. What do you suppose God wanted to teach Elijah here?

Pray

Almighty, infinite Father, I want to know You more! Open my eyes to see You. Awaken my heart to trust You. Open my ears to hear You.

I want to be more aware of Your presence, Lord. I stretch out my hands with a sincere and seeking heart, and I ask You, Lord, to reveal Yourself to me in ways I've not yet experienced. Show me what holds me back. Show me what in my life blocks my view of You. Move my mountains into the sea. Convict me of habits that hinder me. Give me a hunger for the things of God. You promised to draw near when I draw near to You. I'm seeking, waiting, watching, and believing. I want to know You in a way that forever changes me. Blessed are those who wait for You. My soul longingly waits for You. In Jesus' name I pray, amen.

Respond

Pick one of the stories you studied in the reflection questions and return to it several days in a row. Ask God to reveal something new to you. Ask Him to open the eyes of your heart.

Spend some time pondering your history with God. Write down those moments when you most sensed God's presence. Where were you when that happened? What state of mind were you in? How did those encounters impact you moving forward?

Sit with God for a bit and smile at the thought of Him smiling back at you.

Trust His love. Rest in His care. Honor Him with all that you are.

Ponder His Presence

How Should God's Presence Impact Us?

I fear we've gotten so used to living without a sense of God's presence that we've lost our sense of awe. When God moves in close and reveals a measure of His majesty, even the strongest men fall like dead men. Let's look at a few instances from Scripture when God invaded earth in a way that changed everything.

Consider the Mount of Transfiguration. Jesus invited Peter, James, and John to the mountain to be alone. Let's read what happened.

> As the men watched, Jesus' appearance was transformed so that his face shone like the sun, and his clothes became as white as light. Suddenly, Moses and Elijah appeared and began talking with Jesus.
>
> Peter exclaimed, "Lord, it's wonderful for us to be here! If you want, I'll make three shelters as memorials—one for you, one for Moses, and one for Elijah."
>
> But even as he spoke, a bright cloud overshadowed them,

and a voice from the cloud said, "This is my dearly loved Son, who brings me great joy. Listen to him." The disciples were terrified and fell face down on the ground.[1]

When God's voice thunders on earth, we go facedown in awe and wonder. Let's look at another instance from Scripture. Jesus and His disciples gathered at an olive grove, the garden of Gethsemane. The leading priests and a contingent of guards (possibly five hundred men) came to arrest Jesus. Did they really need that many men? There weren't enough men on the earth to arrest Jesus if He decided to oppose them. But He gave up His life willingly. Read what happened:

> Jesus fully realized all that was going to happen to him, so he stepped forward to meet them. "Who are you looking for?" he asked.
>
> "Jesus the Nazarene," they replied.
>
> "I AM he," Jesus said. (Judas, who betrayed him, was standing with them.) As Jesus said, "I AM he," they all drew back and fell to the ground![2]

Try to imagine the scene. Jesus and His disciples were gathered in the olive grove. They heard heavy footsteps, an army, coming their way. Peter took his battle stance. The others braced for a fight. Then Jesus stepped forward. He asked who they were looking for. When He said, "I AM he," the sheer force of His presence knocked five hundred trained soldiers to the ground. Imagine being one of those soldiers. You wonder what just happened. You get up and brush yourself off. And you realize you're clearly outmatched.

At the very breath of God, men fall prostrate whether they want to or not.

These are just glimpses of that glorious day when Jesus returns, when *every* knee will bow and every tongue will confess Him as Lord, whether they've previously acknowledged Him as Lord or not.[3]

But we choose to bow now.

Prayer

Lord, I bow low, open my hands, and declare You King. Help me to live a life worthy of Your name. Amen.

five

God Lavishes Grace

You Can't Earn What You Need Most

The best way to get these identity truths into our hearts is to replace our warped mirrors and beliefs with the truth of God's Word. Most of us carry plenty of misbeliefs about our own value, forgetting how much God sacrificed for our redemption and freedom.

CHIP INGRAM

Recently, I woke up from a vivid dream that I sensed held some insight for me. I reached out to Lynn, one of our most trusted prayer warrior friends. After sitting with the dream and asking the Lord to confirm her thoughts in His Word, she shared her perspective. First, let me tell you about the dream.

I was at a camp/resort of some kind. I wasn't on staff, but I felt entirely at home in this place. I knew my way around the camp and spilled over with joy just to be there. Suddenly a group of newbies filed in and sat down at a long table in the restaurant, which had an up-north feel (varnished tree logs for benches, etc.). Since no staff members were available, I grabbed some menus and program information and ensured each person had what they needed. I welcomed them and gave them the rundown on their time at camp. Then I took their drink orders.

Here's the part that makes me laugh. I was so happy in the dream that when I walked away from the table to retrieve the drinks, I pushed off one table and did a pirouette, then I kicked my leg high and did a flip. Like a ninja-gymnast-athlete, I bounced from table to table and executed flips and twists with grace and strength. I was in my element.

Simultaneously, I kicked high in the air and saw my reflection in a rickety old mirror on the wall at the far end of the room. The darkened glass rippled a distorted reflection back to me. I couldn't believe what I saw. I looked weak and out of shape, and my high kick was an embarrassment. I stopped my joyful dancing and was all at once negatively self-aware. I wondered, *Is this what I really look like?*

But then, something deeper roared within me: *The mirror lies. It's not telling you the truth!* I thought, *I know I kicked my leg high in the air and landed with great strength. I was there.* And then I woke up.

Later, my friend Lynn said, "Susie, this is such a picture of what happens when we move in the power and grace of the Lord Jesus Christ! You were your best self in your dream, serving among your people, the ones God has assigned to you. You were joyful and strong because God is the strength of your heart, and He has healed you in so many ways. His Spirit alive in you allows you to be the best version of who He created you to be. The way you danced and leaped between the tables fits who you are and how you are. The rickety mirror on the far wall represents an outdated perspective of yourself. Susie, you'll never fulfill all of God's highest purposes for you if you're taking your cues from your own perspective of yourself. But as you keep your eyes on Jesus, He'll fill you, give you joy, and empower you to do everything He's created you to accomplish. Where you fix your gaze makes all the difference. As you often say to me, God gets to decide what's true about you, since He's the one who made you."

God's Presence Is God's Grace

God's presence *is* God's grace. That we get to serve Him with gifts He entrusts to us is a profound privilege. That we can enter His presence with boldness and thanksgiving, knowing He's glad to see us, is an unmerited gift of favor. That we can stumble into His presence with a broken heart and a runny nose from crying for hours is a treasure we can't fully measure. We'll never find our Father exasperated by our weakness. We'll always find that our Abba pours His glory and His strength into those places we'd rather hide.

> We'll never find our Father exasperated by our weakness. We'll always find that our Abba pours His glory and His strength into those places we'd rather hide.

Does it feel contradictory to rightly revere God *and* bumble into His presence with our messy selves? Grace allows us to be who we are before a most holy God. And that same grace empowers us to see Him for who He really is: the star-breathing Creator of the universe who is all-knowing, all-powerful, all-majestic in splendor, and all-in when it comes to you.

There'll be moments when His awesomeness drops you to your knees and you see Him in a way that makes you tremble. There'll be other times when He moves in close, right when you're in the middle of a self-berating thought. He'll lift your chin, breathe life into your weary soul, and remind you to take your cues from Him. Could we be more blessed?

We're saved by grace, through faith, not of ourselves; it's a gift from God. Not a result of all kinds of striving or performing. So no one can boast about being a part of God's royal family.[1] We've been grafted into a royal lineage because of what Jesus accomplished on the cross. We receive because we believe. But it's Jesus who paid the price, won the war, and set captives free. He paid for our freedom. He secured our eternity. There's not a Christian on the planet who earned their way. We're saved by grace through faith. What a gift!

> And God is able to make all grace abound toward you, that you, always having all sufficiency in all things, may have an abundance for every good work.[2]

Based on the original translation of the key words *grace, abound, sufficiency, abundance,* and *work,*[3] this passage could be translated this way:

> God is beyond able to lavish His favor and goodness upon us: His goodwill, pleasure, delight, kindness, mercy, wisdom, knowledge, and affection; His capacity to draw us to Himself;

His promise to offer us strength for the task. He is able and more than willing to pour out His goodness on us with great abundance until we're overflowing. He intends that we, having all we need in every situation, will overflow with love, good deeds, and lavish generosity for the world, in whatever sphere He assigns to us.

Jesus, Our Great Shepherd

I love grace stories. Parables that describe God's lavish love for us; word pictures that convey our profound need for Him. Here's one such story:

There once was a shepherd whose life's work was to care for his sheep. He loved them all. Even the little lamb who was especially prone to wander. One day the little lamb distractedly meandered from the group and lost her sense of direction. She looked back to see if anyone had followed her just as she stepped right into a bush of thickets and thorns. She twisted and turned and tried to break free, but it only made things worse. Pain pierced her skin. Trickles of blood spilled down her coat. Panicked, she jerked her leg back hard and heard a snap. Tears escaped her eyes as she trembled in misery and crumpled into a heap. She cried out for help, but no one came to her rescue. Exhausted from it all, she fell asleep.

Suddenly she felt a gentle hand on her head. She looked up to see her shepherd! He smiled tenderly at her. He untangled her from the thickets. Then he carried her across his shoulders back to the fold with great compassion and care. She spent most days nestled across his shoulders in the weeks that followed while the shepherd tended the sheep. His gentle strength comforted her. The power of his steps assured her. She noticed how often he laughed and enjoyed his little lambs. She grew especially attached to the shepherd and wondered why she so often wandered from him. Near to her shepherd was where she was always meant to be.

Different Ways to Wander

When we think about the wanderer, we often imagine decadent indulgence and blatant sin, like the prodigal son. But there are other ways to wander.

I've worked in radio for over sixteen years. I've interviewed high-profile leaders who experienced high-profile disgrace when their private choices went public. I always found it interesting how reports said they *fell from grace*. Is that true? I'm not saying sin is irrelevant (we'll talk about that in a bit). However, if where sin abounds, grace abounds more, can your sin exclude you from grace?

> God's law was given so that all people could see how sinful they were. But as people sinned more and more, God's wonderful grace became more abundant. So just as sin ruled over all people and brought them to death, now God's wonderful grace rules instead, giving us right standing with God and resulting in eternal life through Jesus Christ our Lord.[4]

When Paul talked about our capacity to fall from grace, he wasn't talking about our sin but our tendency to strive—to earn our own way, to perform our way into God's good graces, which we can't do.

For if you are trying to make yourselves right with God by keeping the law, you have been cut off from Christ! You have fallen away from God's grace.[5]

I was the little lamb in that story. My wandering ways led me to strive in my own strength to earn my way and prove my worth (even though, in my head, I knew Christ had paid that price for me). I don't think I'm alone in this struggle. I don't believe that God gave me Lyme disease, but He did allow it. And had He not, I'd likely be a highly functional pharisee.

Instead, that wretched disease compelled me to cling tightly to Jesus. He became my everything. He carried me for miles. My heart learned to beat in rhythm with His. I soon understood that any gift from His hand pales in comparison to the treasure of knowing His heart. I developed an intolerance for distance from Him. I couldn't make it through my day without connecting with Him, seeking Him, and acknowledging His very real presence in my life. It's become a lifelong practice. I've learned that the best thing about my life is *Him*. Nothing matters more than our oneness with God. Nothing.

Why are we so averse to grace? Sometimes it's because we're afraid. We may have a scarcity mindset embedded in our soul and think we're doing everyone a favor by handling most of the work ourselves.

Or we may shun grace because we want to earn our way and it's hard to be so needy.

But the truth is, no matter our reason for struggling to receive grace, we're all more desperate than we know. Someday, when we see our Savior face-to-face, for at least a flickering moment we'll realize that the pain of our sin ran deeper than we knew, the

> **Someday, when we see our Savior face-to-face, for at least a flickering moment we'll realize that the pain of our sin ran deeper than we knew, the impact of our choices cost more than we realized, and the abundance of His grace was far greater than we imagined.**

impact of our choices cost more than we realized, and the abundance of His grace was far greater than we imagined.

We'll fall on our faces before Him in awe, thanksgiving, and overwhelming gratitude. We'll suddenly comprehend with utter clarity just what we've been forgiven of and just how priceless Jesus' victory is to us.

And it's not to say we don't have skin in the game. We do. Our part matters deeply. Ours is to believe and receive, to trust and obey, and to grow in the knowledge of God. It's to become like Jesus through the power of the Holy Spirit mightily at work within us, that we might love as He loves, live as He lives, say what He'd say, pray as He'd pray, and give generously as He so generously has given much to us.

Grace Doesn't Just Save Us; Grace Empowers Us

Grace doesn't just save us; it empowers us. We don't approach our starting block with grace and then leave grace behind to run our race. We need His empowering favor and provision every step of the way. Grace also heals our perspective of ourselves. We stop trying to earn our way and grow more eager to learn what we've been missing. Grace awakens us to God's goodness, puts a spring in our step, and makes us spiritual ninjas. Grace allows us to serve in humbling ways without it ever diminishing our value. It invites us to accomplish great things without it ever going to our heads. Grace fuels us to give when we'd rather hoard, engage when we'd rather self-protect, and receive when we'd rather hide our needs and pretend we're okay.

God's grace invites us to be who we were always meant to be.

Grace says everything that ever needed to be done has been done for you already. Grace says you can finally lay the burden down, let the people who hurt you off the hook—even let yourself off the hook. Grace says there's nothing else you have to do to make yourself right or righteous—that the only response God expects from you in response to His radical forgiveness is to come on home where you belong. Grace says you get to start over. Grace says you get to be free. . . .

You aren't asked to do anything about it—except believe. Put all your weight down on grace and the God who offers it. Accept it. Live in light of it; live as if you can really trust it.[6]

Grace Upon Grace

For every time the Enemy managed to harass or steal from us, we've received a thousand graces from God: Consistent new-morning mercies. Faithfulness at night. The living Word of God at our fingertips. Food on our table. Friends to call when we need them. Worship music to usher us into God's presence. Moments of solitude to reflect on His words to us. Simple joys of journeying with God and the assurance that we'll never walk alone. A beautiful walk along the trails. A sleigh ride through the snow. That one Christmas morning when you were all together for the holiday. The privilege of partnering with God on the earth and the promise that we'll prevail through our battles. A day that turned out surprisingly well. And that one catastrophe that you miraculously avoided. The Holy Spirit's continual work within you and the promise of transformation all around you. The idea that God would confide in you and tell you things you'd otherwise never know or understand.

You've got guardian angels to guard and guide and intervene when you're not even aware. Answers to prayers you've long forgotten but that God remembers. The absolute ironclad promise that Jesus has forgiven all your sins and tossed them into the sea of forgetfulness. And that He is, right now, preparing a place for *you* that will take your breath away. You won't remember the hardships or the hurts because you'll be caught up in the wonder of God's goodness and love. That day is coming.

Oh, what grace. Oh, the love of Jesus!

> From his abundance we have all received one gracious blessing after another. For the law was given through Moses, but God's unfailing love and faithfulness came through Jesus Christ. No one has ever seen God. But the unique One, who is himself God, is near to the Father's heart. He has revealed God to us.[7]

Jesus' presence on earth showed us what God is like. Jesus confronted the power grabbers and defended the vulnerable. He cared deeply about the sick and went to heroic lengths to save the lost. Jesus forgave sinners and restored the outcasts. He stayed in pace with God's grace and only did what the Father told Him to do.

I imagine He smiled and laughed a whole lot. And cried too. He grieved over stubborn unbelief and rejoiced when He encountered bold, courageous faith. He stayed focused on the mission yet had time for weddings, funerals, and a good meal with friends.

He cares about His sheep and will leave the ninety-nine to find the one, even if her mess is her fault. He doesn't run out of grace. There's no end to His love. He offers His heart, His home, and His family to us if we'll only trust that He is who He says He is and follow Him.

Maybe your repeated sin is indulgence, and you hate yourself every time you crawl out of the ditch of despair. Or perhaps your sin is striving in your own strength because it feels impossible to rest in God's care. And you like the accolades you receive when you perform.

No matter who you are or what your sinful bent, know this: there's always more grace for you. If you are in Christ, you've got access to an ocean of grace that's too big to swim across and too deep to be measured.

What About Sin?

People don't like to talk about sin these days. But sin is real and more destructive than we know. And unaddressed sin is what separates us from God. That's why Jesus came. To die for our sin. Does that mean everybody's saved? No. It's only by grace, through faith, that we're saved.[8] But what if the professing

Christian continues to live a *boldly sinful* life? The apostle John said that's not possible. Not that we never stumble and fall, but with the Spirit of Christ alive in us, we change. Our tastes change. What we once thought was funny isn't so funny now. Even so, some of God's precious children spend their lifetime falling into the ditch, crawling out of the ditch, and thanking God for His mercy, only to find themselves in the ditch again.

There's a big difference between someone who blatantly, repeatedly sins and someone who brokenly sins. One thumbs his nose at God with no fear of repercussion, while the other struggles with self-hatred, condemnation, and brokenness. I dare say there are plenty of believers who died more broken than whole, and who were completely restored the minute they beheld their Savior's face.

I've noticed that the closer I walk with Jesus, the more His light shines in my heart. The more I mature in my faith, the more sinful I realize I am. Not in a condemning way but in a revelatory way. Our self-sins run deep, even though we don't always see them. That's why King David prayed prayers like these:

> Search me, O God, and know my heart;
> test me and know my anxious thoughts.
> Point out anything in me that offends you,
> and lead me along the path of everlasting life.[9]
> How can I know all the sins lurking in my heart?
> Cleanse me from these hidden faults.
> Keep your servant from deliberate sins!
> Don't let them control me.
> Then I will be free of guilt
> and innocent of great sin.

May the words of my mouth
and the meditation of my heart
be pleasing to you,
O LORD, my rock and my redeemer.[10]

⌇

*There are also bodies in the heavens and bodies on the
earth. The glory of the heavenly bodies is different from
the glory of the earthly bodies. The sun has one kind of
glory, while the moon and stars each have another kind.
And even the stars differ from each other in their glory.
It is the same way with the resurrection of the dead. Our
earthly bodies are planted in the ground when we die,
but they will be raised to live forever. Our bodies are
buried in brokenness, but they will be raised in glory.
They are buried in weakness, but they will be raised in
strength. They are buried as natural human bodies, but
they will be raised as spiritual bodies. For just as there
are natural bodies, there are also spiritual bodies.*

1 CORINTHIANS 15:40–44

⌇

When I dare pray, "Search me, O God, and know my heart," He does. Sometimes He'll point out areas that I'm already aware of but need to consider afresh, and sometimes He'll touch on something I thought was a strength or a virtue. Never with condemnation. Always with a loving invitation to be made new.

We live in a culture where "anything goes," but that's not the way of the kingdom, and this mindset won't fly with God on the day of judgment. We'll all give an account of our lives—even believers. But it'll be different for us than for those who reject Christ. We'll have to answer for how we stewarded our time, treasure, and talents. Did we bury them in fear? Live like practical atheists? Take God's grace and mercy for granted?

True believers are bothered by their sin. They feel convicted when they violate their conscience or betray God's Word. Those who insincerely profess Christ but live however they want feel no inner wince when they sin. They may have said a prayer with their mouth without meaning it in their heart. Jesus Himself said that there'll even be people who perform miracles in His name who are not legitimate members of the family.

We're assigned our time on earth for eternity's sake, not for our comfort and convenience or to live our own way now and ask for God's blessing later. We serve a holy, majestic God. He's righteous, magnificent, pure, and powerful. He's not one to be trifled with. Yet He continually invites us into a deep, rich relationship with Him.

If we blur the lines of our own sin while holding the rest of the world to a different standard, we'll answer to God. We're not representing God's heart if we blatantly render verdicts against others while giving ourselves a pass. We can know His Fatherly discipline is on its way. He disciplines those He loves.

Here's what's true for the sincere Christ-follower. You love Jesus. You walk with Him. You love His Word, and you listen for His voice. His Spirit works within you, proving and affirming that you belong to Him. As Romans 8:15–17 tells us,

> So you have not received a spirit that makes you fearful slaves. Instead, you received God's Spirit when he adopted you as his own children. Now we call him, "Abba, Father." For his Spirit joins with our spirit to affirm that we are God's children. And since we are his children, we are his heirs. In fact, together with Christ we are heirs of God's glory. But if we are to share his glory, we must also share his suffering.

His Spirit joins with our spirit to affirm that we belong to Him. We're secure in Him. Furthermore, Paul reminded us later in this chapter not to misinterpret our trials. We may suffer. Endure hardship. Be persecuted. But none of it can ever separate us from the Father's love, and none of it can derail His beautiful plan for our lives.

It's possible and even probable to fear God, walk in His ways, cherish His amazing grace, and still fall on our faces.

We may mess up, fall down, say things we don't mean, and react in ways beneath us. But even as we face the consequences of our choices, we'll never fall out of the Father's love, grace, and mercy toward us. And as faithful followers of Jesus, we'll grow even when we don't realize it. Our trials train us, our mistakes humble us, and our dreams encourage us. He's with us, intimately so, every step of the way. We get to be a work in progress without condemnation. Grace is not license to sin. It's the power to become who God created us to be.

Therefore, since we have been made right in God's sight by faith, we have peace with God because of what Jesus Christ our Lord has done for us. Because of our faith, Christ has brought us into this place of undeserved privilege where we now stand, and we confidently and joyfully look forward to sharing God's glory.

ROMANS 5:1–2

Reflect

1. Read 1 John 1 and consider that this letter was written to Christians. Even in biblical times, some Christians thought they could profess Christ but live the way they pleased. We may reason that we're okay since we're not "doing what *they're* doing." But sin is sin. Selfishness is selfishness. Jealousy is the gateway sin to many other evils. Not that God wants us to be perpetually and fearfully sin-conscious. But neither does He want us to make light of sin, because sin destroys. Sin gives the devil an entrance into our lives. Jesus wants us to be Spirit-conscious, which means we'll be finely in tune with His voice in our ears and His work in our hearts, but we'll also feel His wince in our

souls when we betray our conscience. Write down your thoughts about this idea.

2. Read 1 John 2 and notice that sin often reveals itself in the ways we relate to others (whether we love or not) and the extent that we're tied to the things of the world. John didn't mince words. Verse 28 is especially interesting, given that this letter is addressed to Christians. We know and believe that grace is amazing, wild, and accessible. And it'll change our lives! But it's important to understand that some believers (who sincerely trusted Christ for salvation but repeatedly engage with the world) might lose their courage and shrink back in shame on the day He returns. It'll be a powerful yet sobering day—something we should consider now. Write out your thoughts on this chapter.

3. Read 1 Corinthians 1:26–27 and write a paragraph about your transformation. Who were you, and what were you like when God first called you? What has He done in your life? How have you changed? What do you know now that you didn't know back then?

4. Read Romans 8:1–14 and ponder the difference between those who have the Spirit of God within them and those who don't. Write out the defining characteristics of both.

Pray

Almighty, infinite Father, thank You for sending Your precious Son to die in my place. He paid a debt I could never repay and made a way where there was no way. Because of Jesus, I am loved, redeemed, and alive in You. With my knees on the floor and my hands open wide, I thank You. I'm forever grateful. Thank You, Holy Spirit, for Your presence and movement in my life. Search my heart; show me what I cannot see. Help me lose my taste for that which weakens me. Heighten my sensitivity to Your Spirit. Deepen Your convicting work in my soul. Awaken fresh faith in me. I want to walk humbly, boldly, and confidently in Your presence. I surrender my whole life to You. I want Your will, Your way, for Your glory. Always and forever Yours. Amen.

Respond

Move in a little closer. Dare to go a little deeper with God. Ask Him to search your heart and show you what you cannot see. And then, without a hint of condemnation or self-justification, respond to Him. Count on His love. It'll change you from the inside out.

Ponder His Presence

Is Feeling Good the Same As Feeling God?

As someone who has battled chronic illness my entire adult life, I must say, when I feel good, I feel God. I find myself overwhelmed with the sense of His goodness, that He would grant me moments of energy, strength, and clarity. I've contended for complete healing so long that I'm always aware when I gain even an inch. And I praise Him.

Yes, every good gift indeed comes from above, from the heart of a Father who loves us.[1] We overlook so much of the immeasurable kindness of our Father. Every good and beautiful thing comes from His hand. Our lives would be so much richer if we slowed down long enough to notice the wonder all around us.

When we're operating in our calling, empowered by the Spirit, we can sometimes sense the Father's delight, like He's shouting, "*This* is what I created you for! You are my masterpiece!" When we hold a newborn baby and see a family resemblance, it's a sacred and beautiful moment, and we're overwhelmed with thanks. When cancer patients ring the bell after their last treatment and walk out of that hospital, we're all cheering. And it feels good. God is good!

That said, feeling good isn't always the same as feeling God. Sometimes we find ourselves in the valley of the shadow, with broken hearts and weary souls. We don't feel good. But if we look for God, we'll find Him there. Sometimes we're facedown on the floor, heartsick over our sin or the sin of another. God feels a million miles away. But He's closer than our very breath.

Some folks are walking through the best season of their lives. They make a lot of money. Their kids are doing great. They feel good. But they don't know God. Some chase after things that only *temporarily* satisfy (wealth, status, material goods, substances that numb our senses). But the thing is, these things *do* satisfy for a while. And at that moment, some would say they're on top of the world. They feel good, but they're not feeling God. What they're experiencing is the temporary buzz of overindulgence. Even so, these same people may at times experience a subtle breeze or a beautiful sunset and wonder about things eternal. They sense an invitation to look up. They may not know it yet, but they're encountering the presence of God.

Imagine it's Sunday morning, and two women arrive at church with very different heart postures. One arrives tenderized, ready to meet with God. The worship leader lifts up a shout and invites all to rise. The woman stands up and suddenly senses God's nearness. The first few words of the song confirm what God has been saying to her. Tears escape her eyes, and she raises her hands in praise. A couple of rows back, the other woman rushes in and sits down. When the worship leader calls everyone to stand, she rolls her eyes and mumbles, "I hate it when he manipulates a response from us."

So what was true? That God moved in their midst, or that the worship leader manipulated the response from the people? Could it be that God met the first woman but not the second? Maybe her attitude quenched the Spirit's ability to reach her heart.

Seek the LORD while you can find him.
Call on him now while he is near.
Let the wicked change their ways
and banish the very thought of doing wrong.
Let them turn to the LORD that he
may have mercy on them.
Yes, turn to our God, for he will forgive generously.
"My thoughts are nothing like your
thoughts," says the LORD.
"And my ways are far beyond
anything you could imagine.
For just as the heavens are higher than the earth,
so my ways are higher than your ways
and my thoughts higher than your thoughts."

ISAIAH 55:6–9

When it comes to experiencing God's presence, we have more to do with it than we probably imagine. When we draw near, He draws near.[2] He pursues us, delights in us, and moves heaven and earth to bless us. He's always good and kind and present in our lives. We're the ones who get busy, distracted, and offended. Those who treasure His presence cultivate a continual atmosphere to encounter Him.

Prayer

Precious Father, I want to know You more! Help me to be at home in Your presence in a way that puts my heart at rest. Help me know and believe that Your grace has changed everything for me. I want to live loved, extend grace, and grow by leaps and bounds because of who I am in You. Thank You, Lord. Amen.

six

God Offers Life

Take Him at His Word

You were created in the image of God. You were called to great-ness. You are God's workmanship, a child of the King, and God wants to set you free from anything that's holding you back. God wants you to live in the fullest potential that He has for your life. It's time you get serious about victory now that God has given you the opportunity to ask, How is the opposition coming against me? What is the Enemy doing to me? What adjustments can be made?

LOUIE GIGLIO

We pulled up to a house I'd never seen to meet a couple I did not know. Our friend Tami met us at the curb, smiled warmly, and walked with us to the front door. Maria (the tall, angel-like woman I referenced in chapter 3) greeted us and welcomed us into her home. We each found our places on the comfortable couches in the family room, and Maria's husband, Scott, pulled out a notepad. "Tell us your story," he said.

I looked up at my husband, swallowed hard, and started with my first traumatic memory. Step-by-step, I walked them through my story. With my hands folded tightly in my lap, I cautiously looked up at Maria and Scott, feeling sick about how vulnerable I felt. Though I saw only tenderness and care, I wanted to run and hide.

Maria sensed my vulnerability and reached for my hand and gave it a squeeze. She looked me in the eyes and said, "Susie, I know this was hard for you, but we needed to hear the whole story to discern the theft that has taken place in your life. The Enemy always plays by patterns. In every story, you'll find a pattern of theft, a predictable way that he has planted lies and paved inroads so he can repeatedly steal from unsuspecting souls. He started after you when you were a young child. He trespassed in your life at your most vulnerable moments." And that was true. No wonder I lived bracing for impact. Even though I had parents who loved me and a husband who loves me, I never felt safe or protected. Anything could happen at any time, or so I believed.

Maria continued, "Satan often gets away with stealing from God's children what belongs to them. He's a liar and a thief. That's who he is and what he does. He will embezzle wherever he can, but we have a say in this matter as children of God. We're here to discern the theft that's taken place so we can go boldly after the restitution that's owed to you. We want to help you understand all you possess in Christ Jesus because of what He accomplished at Calvary. The thief comes to steal and kill and destroy. But Jesus came that you may have life and have it in abundance. But if you don't know what's yours, you won't know when it's been stolen. You're going to take back what the enemy has stolen. You're about to come into a new awareness of who God really is and what He has for you. And you're going to find a new normal that includes abundance, goodness, mercy, and joyful expectancy. Not to say we don't go through difficult times; we do. But we can go through those times with our spiritual identity intact and God's promises at our fingertips. Remember what the psalmist said? *Surely only goodness and mercy follow me. Surely, they do!* If you don't live with a sense of expectancy, wondering what good thing God is up to in and around you, that's a sign that you need healing, truth, and renewed perspective. It's proof that something is out of alignment in your belief system. Theft pulls us out of alignment. It's the truth that sets us free."[1]

> Remember what the psalmist said? *Surely only goodness and mercy follow me. Surely, they do!* If you don't live with a sense of expectancy, wondering what good thing God is up to in and around you, that's a sign that you need healing, truth, and renewed perspective.
>
> MARIA ERICKSON

We Have to Feel It to Heal It

We'll never fully heal from our experiences if we downplay our hurts. And remember, we can have the humility to own our sins when we truly believe that Jesus paid for them. We'll have the courage to face our fears when we know we don't face them alone. We'll have the resolve to delve into our past trauma when we know there's healing on the other side. God is the Gentle Healer. God is ever-present. God is with you.

If we don't take inventory of our stories and the lies we picked up when life let us down, we won't know how to shore up our lives in the future to prevent enemy theft. Why? Because we'll not discern the Enemy's pattern of intent against us.

If every good gift comes from God, does that mean that every bad thing is from the Enemy? While I don't want to give the Enemy more credit than he deserves, neither do I want to downplay his role in our lives. Adam and Eve started out in a perfect garden, enjoying beautiful fellowship with God and bountiful provision from His hand. How did they fall? The Enemy set the bait, and they took it.

We live in a broken world. Whose fault is that? The Enemy's. And ours. And everybody else's. Satan repeatedly sets the bait, and we frequently fall for his tricks. The result? Hurt people hurt people. Fallen people make others stumble. And all the broken-down walls give the Enemy easy access to our souls.

The harassment you endure while getting ready for Bible study? I'd say the Enemy is behind it. Your tendency to grab things for yourself because you didn't trust God to provide? I'd say the Enemy planted the thought; you let it take root and then reacted in fear. The mean teacher you had in fourth grade who repeatedly talked to you like you were in the way? Not to say that the Enemy positioned her in your life, but he saw an opportunity to plant lies in your tender young heart, and he took it.

In my opinion, he *is* behind every bad thing, whether directly or indirectly. Sin entered the world through man because of him, and his whole aim is to steal, kill, and destroy. We give him way too much access to our stories. We endure some of the hurts we experience because of the brokenness in others. Some we initiate because of our own brokenness. Still, Satan purposely orchestrates other scenarios because he's threatened by us. Sometimes tragedy falls on us through no fault of anyone; it's just a part of life on a broken planet. But whenever the Enemy finds an opportunity for theft, he'll rush in and take it.

Do We Bide Our Time? Or Believe God for More?

How do we recover what's been lost? Do we hold out until heaven? Bide our time until then? Or are there things God wants to restore in the here and now? I believe heaven will take our breath away. We'll experience a sensory explosion that our finite minds cannot imagine. We'll see Jesus face-to-face, in all His glory. We'll breathe heaven's crisp, clean air, and our hearts will come alive with freedom and love. We'll suddenly be free from all enemy opposition and irritation. We'll dance for joy, amazed at all Jesus won for us. We'll be reunited with loved ones and reconciled with old friends. We'll enjoy a feast of epic proportions and unhindered fellowship with God's people. We'll realize that Jesus was so much more excellent than we knew and far kinder than we imagined. Oh, what a day it will be!

But here and now, we feel pain. We get hurt. The Enemy steals from us even though God has made promises to us. Do we have a say in the matter? Can we lay hold of the things that God has promised but the Enemy has stolen? Do we even know what God has promised us? How many of us have thought that salvation only applies to our eternal destiny? If it *were* only that, it would still be a marvelous gift—it would be everything. But the word "saved" implies far more than many of us have understood. Let's unpack a familiar passage we use when speaking of *saving* faith.

> God *saved* you by his grace when you believed. And you can't take credit for this; it is a gift from God. Salvation is not a reward for the good things we have done, so none of us can boast about it. For we are God's masterpiece. He has created us anew in Christ Jesus, so we can do the good things he planned for us long ago.[3]

The Greek word translated as *saved* in this passage is *sozo*, which means "to make well; heal; restore to health; to preserve one who is in danger; to rescue; to deliver from the penalties of judgment."

This passage beautifully reflects the way Jesus lived during His days on the earth. He deeply cares about the human condition. Everywhere Jesus went, He healed the sick, delivered the oppressed, and preached that the kingdom of God was at hand. He came to heal hearts, save souls, and destroy the devil's works. He came to set captives free and then mobilize each of us into someone we never dreamed we could be. He bore our sin and shame and gave us His glory and grace by taking our place. He paid our debt, allowing us to be grafted into His royal family. He makes beauty out of ashes. He brings songs out of sorrow. He gives gladness where there's sadness. He gives joy, inspires hope, and calls us to faith.

We've established that the devil is all about theft. John 10:10 reminds us that Jesus is all about *life*: "The thief approaches *with malicious intent*, looking to steal, slaughter, and destroy; I came to give life with joy and abundance" (THE VOICE).

A life of abundance isn't the same as the health-and-wealth gospel. I've been dirt-poor, and I've had money in the bank. It wasn't until my soul was set free that I realized the Enemy had no claim on me. You can't buy what Jesus offers for free. You can't jump high enough to grab it or perform well enough to deserve it. The kind of peace, wholeness, and freedom Jesus won is a *supernatural gift* that defies our circumstances and that we possess by faith.

Why? Because it's who He is! Jesus *is* love, joy, peace, patience, kindness, goodness, faithfulness, gentleness, and self-control. He's our Healer, Savior, Deliverer, Defender, Advocate, Refuge, Rock, Shelter, and Comfort. When we're intimately aware of Jesus' presence, we become keenly aware of the different aspects of His character, which never change but are emphasized to us based on our need.

Jesus broke the Enemy's claim on us at the cross. Scripture tells us He did even more than that. Jesus made a public spectacle of the Enemy and the powers that oppose us.

> You are an heir with Christ of God's estate. He has placed his Spirit in your heart as a down payment. What God said to Joshua, he says to you: "Every place that the sole of your foot will tread upon I have given you." But you must possess it. You must deliberately receive what God so graciously gives.[2]
>
> MAX LUCADO

Do you think He did that for Himself? He has nothing to prove and no complex that compels Him to vindicate Himself. No. Jesus served the Enemy notice, declaring that salvation, deliverance, freedom, and wholeness are *now* available to us. Jesus is God. He's the second person of the Trinity. His Spirit is alive and active in the lives of believers all over the world. God's presence hovers and moves and intervenes when we're often unaware.

The good news is *so* much better than we first imagined. And I'd say that we possess freedom and fullness in increasing measure to the degree that the lies within us are displaced. Not that His love expands or that we're somehow more saved as we go. But undoubtedly, there are varying levels of freedom, health, and wholeness that we've all yet to lay hold of. If we don't believe it, we'll never contend for it.

Freedom is what Jesus died for! Aware that the Enemy is bent toward destruction, Love came down on a rescue mission. And those who receive Him have the right to become sons and daughters of the Most High God. The thought of it takes my breath away.

You will show me the path of life,
In Your presence is fullness of joy,
At Your right hand are pleasures forevermore.

PSALM 16:11 (NKJV)

We Can Encounter Christ's Power and Provision

In my book *Fully Alive: Learning to Flourish—Mind, Body, and Spirit*, I explore how what happens in our souls happens in our cells. It's just true. Our bodies respond to what our souls have endured. And though I don't espouse the name-it-claim-it, what's-in-it-for-me "gospel" message (which is *not* the gospel), I do believe with all my heart that Jesus cares deeply about your broken heart. He wants to bless the work of your hands. He intends to provide for your needs. He'd love for your children to thrive and for you to engage in the kingdom work He assigns to you. He wants you to speak to your mountains, put fear under your feet, and help others get free. There's nothing self-serving about any of those desires.

When we treat Jesus as a means to an end (instead of the Beginning and the End), our motives go awry. He's not a blessing machine; He's the King of kings. We serve His purposes, not the other way around. But if we're sincere followers of Christ and begin to relate to God in a self-serving way, like the good Father He is, He'll discipline and direct us. His rod and staff will comfort, correct, guard, and guide us. He doesn't shame us. He uses our journey to shape us. We're all a pile of contradictions. But Jesus knew full well who He was saving when He died on that cross. He considered *you* the *joy* set before Him.[4]

I marvel at how quick Christians are to accuse one another. And I marvel at how gracious God is to forgive us and use us regardless of what others say about us.

Based on Jesus' character and His promises, I believe we're on solid biblical ground to pray with confidence, believing that He'll answer prayers like these:

- Jesus, rescue me from my enemy who is too powerful for me![5]
- Jesus, set my feet on solid ground and put a new song in my heart![6]
- Jesus, heal my soul, and make me whole! Heal my body that I might serve You with robust health and strength![7]
- Jesus, I'm done being bullied by my fears; awaken me to faith! Help me to live with power, love, and a sound mind![8]
- Jesus, I refuse to accept insomnia as a way of life. You grant sleep to those You love, and I *know* You love me![9]
- Jesus, I reject insecurity and embrace my God-given identity. You made a masterpiece when You made me and created me for a distinct purpose. I'm an original! Open my eyes to see what You see and to do what You want me to do.[10]
- Jesus, I'm walking through the valley of the shadow right now, but I know You promised to be with me, to prepare a table for me in the presence of my enemies. Nothing can separate me from Your love. Thank You, Lord![11]
- Jesus, I believe You'll supply all of my needs according to Your riches, not mine.[12]
- Jesus, I'm done striving in my own strength. I want to encounter You, Your power, and Your provision in my life![13]
- Jesus, I have a dream for my family that we'll all be actively engaged in Your kingdom and enjoy rich fellowship together. Work wonders in and through us.[14]
- Jesus, I'm burdened for our world today! I want Your good news to upstage the bad news. I'm asking You to cut off the strength of the wicked and increase the power of the godly! I want to dwell in the land and feed on *Your* faithfulness.[15]

- Jesus, I want to reflect Your heart to a desperate world in need. I want to lay hands on the sick so they recover. I want to preach the Word with power.[16]

If you don't know what belongs to you because of Jesus' sacrifice, you won't know what the Enemy has stolen from you because of his greed.

When you were dead in your sins and in the uncircumcision of your flesh, God made you alive with Christ. He forgave us all our sins, having canceled the charge of our legal indebtedness, which stood against us and condemned us, he has taken it away, nailing it to the cross. And having disarmed the powers and authorities, he made a public spectacle of them, triumphing over them by the cross.

COLOSSIANS 2:13–15 (NIV)

Types of Trauma

During my years working in radio, I've had the great privilege of interviewing many incredible leaders. One stands out to me to this day: my interview with Dr. Dan Allender. We talked about his excellent book *Redeeming Heartache: How Past Suffering Reveals Our True Calling*. Dr. Allender has extensive experience in helping people heal from trauma so they can go on to live full lives. After years of working to help people heal, Dr. Allender and his team discovered that all trauma lands in one of three archetypes:

- Orphans: Had to fend for themselves. Often end up being leaders and business owners. High functioning but with a broken heart. They need rest and care.
- Strangers: Always felt on the outside of the circle and out of reach from the powers that be. Tend to struggle with anger, jealousy, and resentment.
- Widows: Endured all kinds of loss (whether an actual widow or not). Identifies with loss and sense of lack.

However, Dr. Allender suggests that when orphans, strangers, and widows heal, they become someone altogether new.

- The orphan becomes a priest—one who advocates for and cares for other orphans.
- The stranger becomes a prophet—one who speaks into the crowd with fresh clarity and conviction.
- The widow becomes royally loved—one who is known by love, saved by love, and who lives loved.[17]

A Healed You

Can you picture it? Maybe you've had an orphan spirit your whole life. But then you encounter God and He shows you what's true about you because of Jesus. Suddenly you become an advocate for others who live like orphans but are actually sons and daughters of the King.

Or maybe you relate to the stranger. You've always felt outside the circle, not a part of the group. What if you dared to lean in and ask God what's true about you? What if He met you with such tender care and power that you began to grasp the importance of your calling? What if instead of anger and frustration, you felt conviction, confidence, and calling? Can you imagine God calling you into circles that were once outside your comfort zone? You open your mouth with skillful and godly wisdom and hearts come alive.

Or maybe you identify more with the widow. You've had a lot of loss in your life. Can you envision what restoration might look like for you? Close your eyes and imagine encountering God's love in a way that seeps into every pore and heals every hurt. Tears escape your eyes, and you start to smile. You're never the same.

These things are possible, you know.

We must acknowledge and prioritize the places within us that need the miracle work of our Savior. The unhealed areas in our lives cause us to misinterpret

> The unhealed areas in our lives cause us to misinterpret our trials, misunderstand God's voice, and miss all the ways He's showing up in our lives.

our trials, misunderstand God's voice, and miss all the ways He's showing up in our lives.

Every story is complex. But in God's presence—when we filter every aspect of our story through the lens of His nearness, sovereignty, and love—our story starts to make sense. Even more than that, our story becomes a beautiful testimony to the redeeming work of God on the earth today.

You can't undo trauma or replace a person who has died. But you can encounter God's presence in a way that heals the wounds, restores the lost years, and redeems the times. He's more than able to do above and beyond all we could ever dare to ask or imagine. His Word says so.

God can do anything, you know—far more
than you could ever imagine or guess or request
in your wildest dreams! He does it not by
pushing us around but by working within us,
his Spirit deeply and gently within us.
Glory to God in the church!
Glory to God in the Messiah, in Jesus!
Glory down all the generations!
Glory through all millennia! Oh, yes!

EPHESIANS 3:20–21 (MSG)

Reflect

1. Look up John 10:10 in several translations and write out a personalized, paraphrased prayer for your life.

2. Read Ephesians 1:3 and note the past-tense words: *has blessed*. He "has blessed us with every spiritual blessing in the heavenly realms because we are united with Christ." This is a profound statement that deserves our attention! Do some word study and searching on your own and learn what it means to be blessed with—to have access to— every spiritual blessing in the heavenly realms.

3. Read Ephesians 1:4–11 and write out some of the benefits of being a child of God. (Remember, Psalm 103:1–5 reminds us to bless God with our whole heart and forget *not* His benefits.) You may count as many as sixteen blessings/privileges depending on your Bible translation.

4. Read Ephesians 1:15–23 and list Paul's desires for his readers. How many did you count, and how did he describe them? Gather Paul's prayer requests for you and write them out in a faith declaration over your life (and even over those you're praying for).

Pray

Heavenly Father, my precious Abba, thank You for sending Your Son to die in my place. And Jesus, thank You for enduring the horrors of hell so that I may enjoy the bounties of heaven. Life forever with You! Fellowship with Your people. Promises fulfilled. Joy unspeakable.

Freedom from pain, tears, and sorrow. Glorious worship and unending awe. I am Yours, and You are mine. Your banner over me is love. Show me the patterns of theft in my life. Open my eyes to see the vulnerable places in my soul. Give me specific promises to shore up my life and shut down the Enemy's access to me. I need healing. Thank You, Lord, that I have a healer! I need wholeness. Thank You, Lord, for You purchased my wholeness. I want to live with purpose. Thank You, Lord, for assigning good work to me. I want everything You won for me. I want my faith to please You and my life to honor You. No more shrinking back in fear. I rise up in faith, knowing You'll make a way for me. In Jesus' name I pray, amen.

Respond

Sit with God, walk through your story, and ask the Holy Spirit to highlight the unhealed places in your life. Open the Bible, read as He leads, and write down what He says.

Look for promises from Scripture that address the broken-down places in your wall that allow the Enemy access. Craft a prayer of biblical promises to shore up your wall and preempt the Enemy's predictable attacks. Remember God's Word. Rehearse His promises. Encourage your soul by pondering His faithfulness.

Sing a song of thanks to God even before your breakthrough comes. Whether you can sense His presence or not, He's right there with you.

Ask God for a vision of what a healed, restored you might look like. Picture it in your mind. And then rise up and allow the Lord to direct your steps.

Ponder His Presence

What Does It Mean to Grieve the Holy Spirit?

Jesus said that when two or more are gathered in His name, He's right there in our midst, with us.[1]

Those with tender hearts respond to God. Some cry out to Him and ask that more of who He is be made known to us. We draw near, and He draws near. But when God moves in close, not everyone is happy about it. Those who refuse to believe that God still moves in our day may step in and quench the Spirit. When this happens, it also grieves the Spirit. But there's more that grieves the Spirit than just a religious spirit. A rebellious spirit breaks His heart too.

Ephesians 4:29–32 says,

Let no corrupt word proceed out of your mouth, but what is good for necessary edification, that it may impart grace to the hearers. And do not grieve the Holy Spirit of God, by whom you were sealed for the day of redemption. Let all bitterness, wrath, anger, clamor, and evil speaking be put away from you, with all malice. And be kind to one another, tenderhearted, forgiving one another, even as God in Christ forgave you. (NKJV)

The word *grieve* in this passage means to cause sorrow, offend, make uneasy, or to distress. If you are sealed with the power of the Holy Spirit, He is alive and at work in you. What a miracle! However, we grieve His heart when we think, act, or say things that God would never say or do. We're made for better things.

Sometimes I get in a hurry, and when a slow driver pulls in front of me, I'll spout frustration in my car. At once, I feel the inner wince. That check in my spirit reminds me that I'm a child of God, called, anointed, and appointed to represent Him. As Christians we're called to a lifestyle of response to the Spirit, not a series of reactions to our circumstances.

We too often presume upon God's favor. He may have gifted us in powerful ways, and we may love it when He works mightily through us. But if our inner world is not wholly submitted to God, if we're flippant about attitudes that grieve His heart and never make a course correction, we destroy our fruit, diminish our influence, and others pay the price. Why? Because the Holy Spirit will not endorse our disobedience. And if He's not in it, our offerings will lack the power they're supposed to have—appointed to have.

It's the Spirit of God—not our fabulous giftings—that changes everything. It's the Spirit of God that convicts us of sin, heals broken bodies, and moves mountains out of the way. It's the Spirit of God that comforts the broken, strengthens the weary, and brings clarity to the obedient. We may wow the crowd with our gifts, but if our offerings are not empowered by the Spirit of the almighty God, we're wasting everybody's time.

R.T. Kendall writes, "When the Holy Spirit is grieved, the anointing lifts. We usually feel nothing at the time. It isn't until some time later that we notice we have carried on out of habit or through the momentum of a natural gift."[2]

Sometimes we grieve the Spirit when we blatantly sin. Other times we cause Him sorrow when we make our plans without consulting His direction and influence. Not because He's insecure, but because we're less secure than we can imagine without the Spirit's direction. The Lord wants to train us to hear His voice. We may feel the nudge to write a letter, make a phone call, or take a different way home from work one day. The more we listen and obey today, the greater our capacity to hear Him when He speaks tomorrow.

Prayer

Lord God Almighty, forgive me for moving so fast that I forget to look to You first. Holy Spirit, awaken me to the reality of Your presence and influence in my life. Help me to be quick to hear and obey. Amen.

seven

God (Sometimes) Seems Silent

Discern the Reason for Your Season

One day, we won't need to trust his love any longer, because we'll be in the presence of our One Great Love. After endless years of trying to see him through the haze and mystery of life's unanswerable questions, we'll finally see him as he's always seen us—face-to-face. On that day, suffering, tears, death, and mystery itself will be no more. The long journey will be over. At last, sons and daughters of God, we'll be . . . home.

KEVIN BUTCHER

I sat cross-legged on the bed in my hotel room, hugged my thick Bible to my chest, and prayed the words I'd just read from the Word.

After months of walking through a dark night of the soul, where God seemed silent and the Enemy obnoxiously loud, I finally felt peace, relief, and rest. Like a jolt of lightning, the sun punched through the clouds and the warmth of God's presence flooded my entire being. I felt loved, seen, cared for, and known. What changed? Had I done something to cause it?

For months the days had felt dreary, the skies cloudy, and God seemed miles away. I longed to hear His voice or sense His nearness or affection. I begged Him to speak.

But nothing.

I fasted, prayed, and worshiped, all into the darkness with no sense of light. While I prayed that my offering meant something to God, I couldn't help but wonder if He'd changed His mind about me.

I retraced my steps, trying to discern if I'd done something to chase Him away. I asked God to search my heart, know me, and show me what I couldn't see. Surely, He'd answer such a prayer! But no. I sensed no conviction or correction. I sensed nothing, which made this season even more painful. I was still a young believer. I wish I had known back then what I know now! But isn't that the way we mature? We learn to walk by faith when there's no sight or seemingly no end in sight.

During that time, several of my friends enjoyed the time of their lives. They were thrilled over breakthrough answers to prayer after only short seasons of struggle. Their kids thrived, their health flourished, and their sense of purpose oozed out of their pores. I was happy for them but sad for me. Was this a test? A punishment? The way God is sometimes? What was I supposed to do in the meantime?

Weeks into this dark season I remembered something I often told my boys when they were young: "Every time you open the Word of God, you open the mouth of God. He speaks mightily through His Word. If you want to discern His voice, get to know His Word." Were those words still true today? They were.

Does my silent season have the capacity to change God's character? No, it doesn't. Still, why must these silent seasons last so long? And what's their purpose in our lives?

I decided to rehearse God's promises and to remember some of the times He spoke to me clearly. I needed to ponder what He'd said back then to see if it made more sense now. Sometimes it did; sometimes it didn't. I went about my life as best I could. I loved my family, served at church, and navigated health challenges, all with a sad heart. I missed God. There was nothing like His presence.

I realized that I was sad because I'd misinterpreted my experience, which caused me to question what I believed to be true. I did my best to stay the course, but I could have gone through my days with a holy expectancy had I known then what I know now. I would have faithfully served, wholeheartedly believed, and continued in my work until the season shifted.

Since then, I've had plenty of similar seasons, and they no longer shake me like this first one did.

I know God is not going anywhere. He promised to get me safely home. So when I can't hear God's voice or sense what He's up to, I remember and rehearse what He's spoken to me in the past. I reread passages I've since memorized. I make sure there's plenty of time and space in my day to listen. When I'm less apt to doubt His love for me, I wait. I worship. And I believe that in due time He will speak.

To Know His Love

Nothing makes sense if God's love doesn't make sense. God's love opens our eyes, ears, pores, hearts, cells, and capacity to trust Him in every season.

Nothing makes sense if God's love doesn't make sense. God's love opens our eyes, ears, pores, hearts, cells, and capacity to trust Him in every season. That's why Scripture says that *to know this Love* is to be filled to the fullness of God. Because of Jesus, we are now anchored, tethered to our good God, and nothing—not anything—will ever separate us from His love ever again.[1]

Passing the Test

It was sixth grade. I hovered over my test, pencil gripped too tightly. I knew the answers but suddenly began to second-guess everything I'd learned. Then I felt the presence of someone standing beside me. I looked up to see my teacher, whose kind eyes put my heart at ease. He smiled, gave me a nod, and continued down the row.

My confidence surged; I determined to finish the rest of the test with a poised assurance. After all, my teacher had done his job. He had taught our lessons with kindness and clarity. This test was simply a tool to prove what we knew, to bring to the surface what had been planted in us.

God doesn't ever tempt us to do evil; that would be contrary to His nature. But He does test us now and then, sometimes to reveal what's in us. He isn't wondering about us, but sometimes we're wondering about ourselves. Certain tests prove how far we've come. We live in our own stories, so we're not always aware of our progress. You're not the person you were five or ten years ago. If you've walked intimately with Jesus, you have more truth in you today than you did yesterday. God sometimes shows you what you know so you'll more firmly trust Him as you go. He's been faithful before. He'll be faithful again.

Other times, God tests us to show us our areas of need and vulnerability—not to expose us but to prepare us for our next assignment. Such tests help us understand the trials we face and the opposition we endure. I've heard these opportunities called "training time for reigning time."

Insecurity compels us to take the wrong things personally. We'll read between the lines and wonder if God's lack of response is intended to hurt us. We suddenly notice when others seem to overlook us, and the hurt goes deeper than it should. We begin to doubt our worth and place in the greater kingdom story.

The thing about these dark nights of the soul is that they're

May you experience the love of Christ, though it is too great to understand fully. Then you will be made complete with all the fullness of life and power that comes from God.

EPHESIANS 3:19

hard, often lonely, and make us wonder if God changed His mind about us (like people sometimes change their minds about us).

We find our footing again by reminding our souls what's true, even when it doesn't feel true. The divine authority we possess in Christ, the love that He has unequivocally demonstrated to us, and the mighty, powerful Spirit of the living God right now at work *within*—these help us to remain confident in our Maker, no matter what kinds of opposition we face or what types of seasons we endure.

And remember, God is still present even if He's silent. He'll not abandon you, turn on you, or gossip to someone about you. Never. Ever. Not in a million years.

> **God is fierce in your defense, consistent with His love, and faithful to His promises. He *will* finish what He started in you. He delights in you. He's grateful to call you His own.**

God is fierce in your defense, consistent with His love, and faithful to His promises. He *will* finish what He started in you. He delights in you. He's grateful to call you His own. That's the unchanging truth about you because of the unchanging love of your invested, interested, involved heavenly Father.

We know our silent seasons have served us well when we emerge from them with a more robust assurance of God's love, a deeper understanding of His Word, and a greater awareness of our place in His heart.

Is This a Trial or an Attack?

"Why won't you fight?" Kev pleaded with me as I curled up in a ball in our bed. "This isn't like you. Go after this like you go after everything else." But I wanted to die. Two of my three sons had wandered from the faith. They drank and partied and posted their pictures on social media. Comments from judgmental Christians left me breathless. I'm an introvert. A homebody. And I'm pretty private. This was agonizing for my soul.

Add to that a deep oppression that covered me like a lead blanket. I couldn't get out from under it. I felt like I was under a curse. In fact, looking back, I believe I was. This wasn't like past seasons where God seemed silent. This felt like a frontal assault straight from hell, and I couldn't fathom how I'd get to the other side of the battle. The Enemy spewed in my ear, "*Everything* you sowed into your sons' lives is gone. *None* of it stuck. They're rejecting you and your faith. All of it was a waste. None of it mattered." With my arms wrapped around my waist, I doubled over and couldn't catch my breath. How could this be? How did this happen? We were so intentional, loving, nonreligious, and profoundly purposeful in our parenting. Our kids would say the same thing. The thought that *none* of what we imparted had stuck sucked the life right out of me. It wasn't true. But it sure felt true.

Writing these words, I see how crazy and blatant these lies were. And even when my sons wandered, they still loved us, had a great work ethic, and were fun and funny and kind. They were just more distant than usual, and we didn't enjoy the fellowship we once had. But the despair and oppression I felt were thick, tangible, and overwhelming. It was demonic.

It took my husband's heartfelt plea for me to realize that this was more than a painful season. I was in the Enemy's crosshairs and needed to rise up and fight back with a ferocious roar. I called some of my praying friends. I cried in their ears and told them I couldn't do this alone. We prayed together on the phone, and then I marched around my house and prayed some more. I put on my armor and stood my ground. I felt strength rise within me. Suddenly, the oppression lifted and fierce faith returned. God had restored my roar. I began to worship God with my heart, declaring my God to be everything He says He is. And in due time, Jesus went after my sons and led them back to a place of sincere faith.

A couple of years ago, my son Luke left his job and started a carpentry company. Six months after he started his company, he decided to study for his contractor's license. He studied thoroughly and prayed passionately. He took many practice tests and circled back to the incorrect answers until he knew the material by heart. Test day came, and he had four hours from start to finish. He walked away feeling reasonably confident that he had passed. He hoped so anyway. A week or two later, he learned that he passed with a 90 percent score. He was thrilled. Then, a week later, he ate something that disagreed with him, and it messed up his system, gave him brain fog, and affected his sleep. Around that same time, he stumbled upon one story after another of successful, experienced contractors who were miles further down the road than he. Luke started to doubt himself and question his decision to go out on his own, even though he had plenty of work going and his customers were happy with him. So what happened? First, Luke took a test. Then he encountered an attack. How do we tell the difference?

Test

- We're stretched and challenged, but if we keep our wits about us, we know we'll have what we need to endure and overcome.
- We're called to up our game and learn new ways of applying what we know.
- We're called to learn new things.
- We're invited to trust God on a whole new level.
- We're tempted to take our eyes off of God and put them on the storm.
- We're tempted to find a way out of the test because it's uncomfortable.
- When we trust God and walk intimately with Him through the test, we supernaturally find a context for the test, which helps us prevail.

Attack

- We endure some physical attack or ailment that weakens us and our resolve.
- We "coincidentally" stumble upon stories of others who thrive where we do not or who have what we long for.
- We're reminded of all the pain and suffering we've endured thus far.
- We're only seconds away from discouragement and despair.
- We lose our will to fight.
- We feel exhausted.
- We can't see the forest for the trees (we lose sight of what's true).

When God tests us, He's proving what's in us and preparing us for His purposes. We need to remember what we know, seek to learn, and pursue God with our heart, soul, mind, and strength.

When the Enemy attacks, we must address it right away. Submit to God, resist the devil, and he *must* flee from you.[2] Don't let the toxins linger in your soul. Call a friend, refute the lies, resist the Enemy, and stand in faith. You can literally turn some battles on a dime when you discern the nature of your trial.

Do note that it's quite possible to walk through a test and an attack at the same time. Your adversary will waste no time to capitalize on an opportunity if he sees one. That's why it's critical to walk intimately with God, to know His ways and His Word, and to be quick to discern the reason for the trouble you're facing.[3]

Silence Is Not the Same As Absence

God promised never to leave us or forsake us. He is always present in our stories. He never gets distracted, looks away, or forgets where we live. He is purposeful in everything He does. He knows us better than we know ourselves.

So if for some reason He seems silent, it behooves us to consider a few things. For starters, God speaks to us in ways that are unique to us. He created us with passions, preferences, and a divine purpose.

He made extroverts and introverts, activists and pacifists, creatives and intellectuals. He loves His spontaneous children as much as those who thrive with a five-point plan. He speaks through His Word, impressions, visions, dreams, and other believers. He even speaks through unbelievers, many times unbeknownst to them.

If we expect God to communicate the same way all the time or try to emulate someone who seems to hear a lot from Him, then we may miss what He's actually saying to us.

One important thing to remember is that He never speaks anything contrary to what we read in His Word. But that said, the way He communicates to each of us may be as unique as we are. It's really a beautiful thing. In his fabulous book *How to Hear God*, Pete Greig writes,

> We often confuse theology with psychology. The fact that God speaks is a matter of *theology*. It's about God's nature. But how we hear God speak is a matter not of theology but of *psychology*. It's about how our neural pathways have learned to receive and process data, which varies from person to person. One individual may indeed be flooded with feelings of peace when they propose to their girlfriend, while another may be utterly terrified. This probably says more about the way that person is wired than it does about the will of God for their lives. . . . Many people struggle to hear God because they have been taught to listen for his voice in ways that are difficult or even impossible for them to process.[4]

If you're interested in exploring this topic further, I highly recommend Gary Thomas's book *Sacred Pathways*. In the book, Thomas suggests that some people deeply connect with God through solitude, while others sense Him when they're out in nature, and still others, through activism. I come alive in solitude, in nature, and on my bike, riding the trails. I sense God's presence, experience His goodness, and am overwhelmed by His love when I'm riding my bike on a hot, sunny day.

Though I love my church and the people in my church, and

our worship times are extraordinary, I most often intimately connect with God in my morning times of prayer. Which makes sense for an introvert like me. How about you?

Embrace the beautiful and unique way God wired you. Trust that He is good and made a masterpiece when He made you. Meet Him in those places and spaces where you feel like the best version of yourself. Thank Him for His willingness to meet you right where you are.

But that's not to say that He won't also show up at your sickbed, messy office, or in your laundry room. Remember, He walks through walls to get to us! But knowing and embracing our unique personalities is an excellent place to start when it comes to hearing God's voice.

Sometimes God seems silent because He's waiting on us. It's our move. He's asked us to do something, yet we've put it off for another day and wonder why we can't hear Him. If it's all crickets when you pray, it's worth pausing to take inventory of your most recent conversations with Him. Have you made promises you intended to keep? Confessed a compromise you've yet to address? God's not holding out on you. But He moves in rhythm with His will. Obedience is a big deal.

Silence Is Not the Same As Darkness

Silent seasons, though unnerving, are survivable. If we can believe who God is and who He says we are and keep sowing, believing, and receiving His love as irrefutable promises from heaven, the clouds will eventually break, and we'll find ourselves strengthened in the Lord in a way that we notice.

On the other hand, demonic attacks feel like they'll swallow us whole. They require action and intervention. If you're walking through a season of oppression, *do not isolate yourself.* Call on the elders of your church or some trusted, godly friends who know how to go to war on your behalf. Allow them to pray for you and fight for you.

This I've learned about such times: Though you need fellow warriors to stand against the Enemy's onslaught against you, and we're far more powerful together than we are on our own, there's a part of this battle that no one can engage in but you. You're the one who needs to put on the armor God has assigned to you. You're the one who needs to stand firmly in faith and refuse to be denied. You're the one who needs a vision for what God has said is true about you. You're the one who decides that you're not backing down because you know what God has promised you, and *this* isn't it! Goodness and mercy will indeed chase after you. You're the one who decides to contend for the life God offers you. Your friends can't care more about your life than you do.

Kara was a member of my coaching group. She wrote:

There's been this one thought that has radically changed my mind about my situation. I hope I explain it right. This earthly life is the only time I will be able to give God my sacrifice of praise. The hurt, confusion, betrayal, grief—every pain I feel here—is the only time in eternity I can give it to Him. Not that He enjoys that I hurt but that I choose to trust Him in it. Maybe that's why He treasures our tears and bottles them. As I stumbled through the first weeks after my life exploded, I regularly heard various versions of, "Trust me, you're going to be okay." He started showing me that He wanted me to think in opposites: forgiveness instead of hate, generosity instead of self-preservation, and the *big* one, rest instead of striving in worry.

Stay open to the idea of God's goodness, even when He seems silent. He's always near, always lovingly teaching us how to trust Him. And when the time is right, He'll punch through the clouds with His healing rays, and we'll remember afresh that we're going to be okay.

Is It Ever Our Fault?

Was it Job's fault that the Enemy ravaged his life? Was it Joseph's fault that he ended up in prison? Was it Jesus' fault that He ended up on the cross? Obviously, no. Righteous men suffered because of sin, darkness, and a very real enemy in all these cases. But is it *ever* our fault when God seems distant? Let's explore what Scripture says.

> Who can be compared with the LORD our God,
> who is enthroned on high?
> He stoops to look down
> on heaven and on earth.[5]

God is omnipresent—which means there's no place where God's power can't go, no depths that His love cannot reach, no height that reaches higher than Him. He stoops down to look at heaven.

> Though the LORD is great, he cares for the humble,
> but he keeps his distance from the proud.[6]

Since there's no place out of God's reach, what does it mean that He *distances* Himself from the proud? Does He turn His back on them? We all have our prideful moments; does that mean He turns His back on us? Let's break down Psalm 138:6. In this case, the New King James Version reads closest to the original translation.

> Though the LORD is on high,
> Yet He regards the lowly;
> But the proud He *knows* from afar.

The Lord is high, holy, pure, and powerful. He draws near and takes great delight in the humble. But He reacts differently to the prideful soul. The key word to focus on in this passage is *yada*, the Hebrew word translated as "knows." Here's how it has been defined: "To perceive. To know by experience. To know intimately. To have knowledge of."[7]

The verse might be paraphrased this way:

Though the Lord God Almighty is highly exalted, far above any earthly thing, He regards with great affection the humble, reverent heart. But those who think more highly of themselves than they ought, those who look down their noses at others, miss out on the privilege of intimately knowing God the way He wants to be known. Their own pride keeps them from seeing themselves in light of eternity. Their skewed perspective keeps them from experiencing and encountering God in a way that could change them.

Does God *go away* when we're full of pride? No. But we may feel distant from Him—because we're the ones who moved. We may sense a lack of presence, peace, or comfort because we've grieved the Spirit. God's power is always flowing, but we put a kink in the hose when we embrace attitudes that are inconsistent with His character.

We get in our *own* way when our hearts go astray. Nothing can separate us from His love. Jesus was a friend of sinners. He died for us, after all. He pursues us when we wander and corrects us when we're wrong. He guards and guides us onto the best path for our lives.

If we blatantly walk away from our convictions, wholeheartedly engage in sinful behavior, and ignore the inner conviction of the Spirit, we will, in due time, face the consequences of our choices. But Jesus even meets us in those places. He doesn't sanction sin, and He never will. But neither will He ever give up on His children.

We may feel the tangible sense of darkness we've allowed in our lives. We may be tormented by the Enemy's minions because we stepped out from under God's loving protection. We may endure unnecessary hardship and life-altering consequences. But if that happens, we're only one prayer away from restored fellowship with our Father.

God doesn't turn His back on us. And if we turn our back on Him, He'll seize every opportunity to provide a way home.

Let's not forget what it means to be a part of the family of God. His mercies are new every morning. His compassions never fail. His promises are secure. And His love will always endure. Take your time and work your way through this powerful psalm. It's for us today.

Let all that I am praise the LORD, with my
whole heart, I will praise his holy name.
Let all that I am praise the LORD, may I never
forget the good things he does for me.
He forgives all my sins and heals all my diseases.
He redeems me from death and crowns
me with love and tender mercies.
He fills my life with good things. My
youth is renewed like the eagle's!
The LORD gives righteousness and justice
to all who are treated unfairly.
He revealed his character to Moses and
his deeds to the people of Israel.
The LORD is compassionate and merciful, slow to
get angry and filled with unfailing love.
He will not constantly accuse us,
nor remain angry forever.
He does not punish us for all our sins, he does
not deal harshly with us, as we deserve.
For his unfailing love toward those who fear him is as
great as the height of the heavens above the earth.

He has removed our sins as far from
us as the east is from the west.
The LORD is like a father to his children, tender
and compassionate to those who fear him.
For he knows how weak we are, he
remembers we are only dust.
Our days on earth are like grass, like
wildflowers, we bloom and die.
The wind blows, and we are gone—
as though we had never been here.
But the love of the LORD remains forever
with those who fear him.
His salvation extends to the children's children
of those who are faithful to his covenant,
of those who obey his commandments!
The LORD has made the heavens his throne,
from there he rules over everything.
Praise the LORD, you angels, you mighty ones who carry
out his plans, listening for each of his commands.
Yes, praise the LORD, you armies of angels
who serve him and do his will!
Praise the LORD, everything he has created,

everything in all his kingdom.
Let all that I am praise the LORD.

PSALM 103

Reflect

1. Think about a time when you felt God had abandoned you. Consider the timing of that moment and the Enemy's intent to steal from you. What did you learn from that experience?

2. Read Hebrews 13:5 and write out a faith declaration based on this verse. Keep it handy if the Enemy ever tries to make you doubt God's love.

3. Think about proximity for a moment. God draws near to the humble. He draws near to the brokenhearted. Can you remember a time when you tangibly sensed His presence? Write it down.

4. Consider Job, right in the middle of the most unimaginable trial. Read Job 19:25–27 and consider that Job made this declaration *before* God restored him. What declaration do you need to make today while waiting for your breakthrough?

Pray

High King of heaven, God of Angel Armies, I know You love me, and I love You! Help me steward Your Word and listen for Your voice as a way of life. I want so much of Your Word hidden in my heart that when I walk through seasons of testing or trial, I'll instinctively know what's true. I confess that I've not always treasured Your voice in my ear. I've not always put a high priority on cultivating an intimate relationship with You. Forgive me, Lord! I want to know You more! I want to hear what You have to say and understand what breaks Your heart. Holy Spirit, awaken a heightened sensitivity in me. Speak in such a way that I know it's You. Help me be quick to obey, quick to forgive, and quick to respond to whatever You say. Help me discern the difference between a test and an enemy attack. I thank You, Lord, that nothing in all creation will ever separate me from Your love. I'm safe in Your care. I trust You with my life, today and forever. Amen.

Respond

Spend extended time with God and ponder your life's story thus far. Look back on your past battles. Ponder the difference between enemy oppression meant to derail you and God-ordained opportunities for forging a beautiful and robust faith.

Write down a few memories from both examples.

Walk with God down memory lane and ask Him to speak to you. What did you learn? What do you know to be true now that you didn't back then? What tests served you well? How much quicker are you to stand firm in the face of an enemy attack? Remember, He works *all* things for the good of those who love Him and are called according to His purpose.[8]

Spend some time thanking God. You're still standing. And He's with you every step of the way.

Ponder His Presence

Is There Anything I Can Do
When God Seems Silent?

Sometimes when walking through what feels like a dark night of the soul, it seems like there's nothing we can do. But there's always something we can do. We can worship (because He's still worthy of our praise). We can pray (because He's still answering prayers). We can engage our faith and grab hold of His promises (because they're all yes and amen).[1]

We can rehearse what we know to be true. Remind ourselves of the truths we often forget. Sing a new song to the Lord while we wait for our breakthrough. Care for our soul by doing some things that breathe fresh life into us. Consider others who are walking through a difficult time and could use a friend.

We can start a thankfulness journal and count every single thing we're grateful for today that we'd miss tomorrow if it went away. Read whole books of the Bible (suggestions: Psalms, Proverbs, the Gospels, Galatians, Ephesians, Philippians, and

Colossians—actually, any book will do). Remind ourselves that God's silence is not the same as absence.

Sometimes God seems silent because He's teaching us to trust Him even when we don't see or sense His involvement in our lives. Sometimes He's speaking, but we're so busy and distracted that we're unable to hear His still, small voice.

When I walk through seasons of silence, I do everything I can to place myself on the path of His promises. I don't want to miss Him. I don't want to be the reason I can't hear Him. Unfortunately, we're not always so good at waiting.

Remember how God used Moses to lead the charge out of Egypt, through the Red Sea, and to the other side? The Israelites were partakers of a history-making miracle! But what happened when Moses ascended Mount Sinai to meet with the Lord? Let's read:

> When the people saw that Moses was so long in coming down from the mountain, they gathered around Aaron and said, "Come, make us gods who will go before us. As for this fellow Moses who brought us up out of Egypt, we don't know what has happened to him."[2]

Wait. What? They had witnessed death-defying miracles before their very eyes! The God of Abraham, Isaac, and Jacob delivered them from captivity, parted the sea, and saved them from certain death. They were there! But because they got tired of waiting for instruction from the Lord, they told Aaron to make them some "small g" gods. And what about their disrespect toward Moses? *As for this fellow Moses (who, by the way, brought us up out of Egypt).* This fellow Moses? In a short amount of time, they'd forgotten about the majesty and power of Almighty God. And they'd diminished their God-appointed leader to that of some fellow they were ready to toss aside.

Moses is on Mount Sinai, a mountain of fire, receiving the Lord's commandments. Picture the dark clouds swirling, thunder rumbling the ground beneath his feet. Moses bows reverently before the Maker of heaven and earth.

Meanwhile, down below, the people go rogue because they're bored and restless. This is such a picture of how easily discontented we can become while God is actively being who He always was and always will be.

If you're in a season of silence, trust the name of the Lord. Guard against discontentedness, unhealthy self-indulgence, and constant distractions. Lean in. Develop a posture of active waiting and purposeful listening. This silent season will pass in due time. Here's your opportunity to grow in trust, solidify your confidence, and engage your faith muscle. It'll serve you well in the days ahead.

Prayer

Lord, You are all I need. I declare with a heart of faith that You are always present, always active, and always involved in my life—even when I can't see You. I trust You, Lord. Amen.

eight

God Matures You

He Reveals, You Respond

Like a tree sends its roots down deep into the subterranean world,
we must learn to tap into the presence of God where he resides
within us, deep in our inmost being.

JOHN ELDREDGE

Our marriage hung by a thread. We both loved Jesus. We loved each other. Well, he still loved me. I no longer felt any kind of love for him. If I'm honest, I felt only contempt, which broke my heart. He never cheated and was never verbally abusive. But he was absent. A workaholic. Killing it at work and serving in multiple leadership capacities at church. A hero to everyone but me. Over the years of our marriage, we'd walked through six- and nine-month stretches where he overworked because of stresses at work and projects that demanded his time. Then we'd have to reset, and he'd make all kinds of promises not to let it happen again.

But this particular stretch had endured for three years. I'd sounded the alarm multiple times, told him this was not sustainable, that I needed his help, his input—and some tender care would be nice too. Kevin is as kind and patient as they come, but for some reason, whenever I broached the subject, his eyes glazed over, like my words couldn't penetrate his focused purposefulness to get the job(s) done. He said later that he believed that, since we had such a strong marriage, we'd be fine. He just needed to get through this busy stretch.

Because I love and fear God, I had no plans to leave. But I prepared to leave him in my heart. Thought about sleeping on the couch. Considered giving him the rubbery piece of chicken for dinner. Is there an acceptable Christian way to make your husband pay for breaking your heart? Apparently not.

One morning (like most mornings), I cried out to God to hear my voice and intervene somehow. I desperately didn't want a dead marriage to be my story.

"God, hear my prayer! Awaken my husband to see what he needs to see. Protect our marriage. Protect our family. I don't know what to do, but my eyes are on You." On my knees with my face in my hands, I begged God to intervene somehow. One day God did just that. He started by confronting me.

I want you to apologize to your husband.

"Uh, what? Why? What have I done? I'm working my tail off trying to keep everything in order at home."

He gently, but with absolute clarity, spoke to me: *I know Kev is missing it right now, but you've committed the greater sin. Kev still really loves you. You've allowed your love to grow cold. Love is the highest order of the day. You promised to love him in all seasons. You need to repent to Me and apologize to him.*

My anger kept the house clean, the laundry done, and the task list to a minimum. I wasn't one to vent my anger; I suppressed it as if it were a superpower. And it was. Unvented anger empowered me in all the wrong ways. My anger was more of a wedge in our marriage than Kev's absence. Though I loved my morning devotional times, laughed wildly at my rambunctious boys, and served at church, my distance from my husband diminished my intimacy with God. That's not to say you can't have a terrible marriage and a fantastic walk with God; you can. But only when you tend to the issues of your own heart.

I prayed, "Lord Jesus, with all my heart, I ask Your forgiveness. I was blind and self-righteous, but now I see."

I felt God's tangible presence as I repented.

So now you need to rethink everything and turn to God so your sins will be forgiven and a new day can dawn, days of refreshing times flowing from the Lord.[1]

I sensed His goodness and kindness and patience. I even felt His smile and affection. He didn't mind that I was feisty. He made me this way. But our strengths can lead us to sin in mere seconds. I realized once again that I needed to trust Him more than I trusted myself or my perspective. I was broken but not destroyed, convicted but not condemned. At that moment God embraced and

> *For God is working in you, giving you the desire and the power to do what pleases him.*
>
> PHILIPPIANS 2:13

empowered me to obey Him. Nothing mattered more than doing the next thing He asked of me.

Though it felt like a costly, vulnerable thing to do—especially with no guarantee that things would ever change—I needed to apologize. That night after dinner, Kev went to the living room to look over a set of blueprints (back before digital copies were available). I stepped into the living room and said, "Hon, can we talk?" Without looking up from his notes, he nodded, "Sure."

I thought it best if I sat on the floor as a humble gesture to my God. I meant business not because I loved my husband but because I feared God and intended to do what He asked of me.

I looked up at the back side of the blueprint and said, "You know these last few years haven't gone the way I'd hoped. We're not doing well. But when I spent time with God this morning, He showed me that I was the one who committed the greater sin."

Kev suddenly looked at me, shocked by my words. I continued, "Though you have missed it, you haven't heard my cries for help these past few years; I know you still love me. Yet I've allowed my love toward you to grow cold. I ask your forgiveness. I made a promise before God to love you in all seasons. So whether or not you get me or change your ways, I will choose to love you, take good care of you, and honor you as the head of this home. Why? Because I love and honor God, and that's what He's asked of me."

Kev's jaw dropped open. Stunned and saddened, he said, "Is *this* what my choices have been doing to you?" The dam broke. I wept with my face in my hands. Kev slipped off the chair and onto the floor to wrap me in his arms.

Things were not all roses and lilies after that. My well had run dry. I didn't have positive feelings about my marriage. But

I had peace with God. And I knew love was a choice. The feelings would come later. Now was my time to obey. There were moments when it seemed he'd stepped back into his crazy work mode, and I was tempted to step back into my frustrated, angry mode. But I remembered my promise to God, so I offered Him my frustration and I laid hold of His peace, grace, and wisdom.

I moved toward Kev, gave his shoulder a squeeze, made him a nice dinner, prayed blessings over the work of his hands, and gave him the fluffy pillow. Every single time I chose love and kindness—especially when it wasn't the instinctive thing to do—I experienced something of God's nearness.

When we set our minds on things above, embrace a perspective based on God's promises (not our problems), and make the fundamental choice to operate in the opposite spirit that our flesh demands, we walk on water. The winds and the rain become irrelevant because we've fixed our eyes on Jesus. Time and time again, the Spirit of the living God within us will defy the gravity of the circumstances around us, if only we trust His way above our own.

> Time and time again, the Spirit of the living God within us will defy the gravity of the circumstances around us, if only we trust His way above our own.

God Matures Us Over Time

Both Kev and I had some things to unlearn so we could find a new rhythm of life that honored God and our marriage. We longed to flourish and be more fruitful than we were experiencing at the time. Two steps forward, one step backward. We got up from that place determined to walk in a deeper level of humility, teachability, and accountability before each other and God. We learned that God is near the brokenhearted, the humbly repentant, and the soul who longs to please Him. Jesus never made a move without the input of His Father. We decided that should be the case for us as well.

I wasn't the only one experiencing God's presence. The more Kev dared to draw some hard lines with his work life and trusted God to do the heavy lifting, the more he *grew* in his faith. His countenance changed. He looked more rested, more grounded. And I fell in love with him all over again. The good days outweighed the bad days. The Spirit of God within us changed everything about us. Now Kev says that his dependence on God *is* his superpower.

Here's my instruction: walk in the Spirit, and let the Spirit bring order to your life. If you do, you will never give in to your selfish and sinful cravings. For everything the flesh desires goes against the Spirit, and everything the Spirit desires goes against the flesh. There is a constant battle raging between them that prevents you from doing the good you want to do.

GALATIANS 5:16–17 (THE VOICE)

Kev and I decided to take a ruthless inventory of our commitments, motivations, fears, hopes, and dreams. We agreed on the nonnegotiables: starting and ending every day with prayer and God's Word; keeping short accounts with our sin and open communication about our hurts; embracing faith-filled generosity as a core value in our marriage; and passionately pursuing God. We longed to know Him more and to make Him known; to help the poor; to get away every year and pray the "impossible" prayer: *Lord, what impossible thing do You want to do through us next?*

We are efficiently managing five times more now than we were during our tough stretch in marriage. And we do so with boundaries and a reasonable bedtime. Not because we've learned the secret of high-level management but because we learned the secret of the abiding life.

What Grows Us

Jesus cares a lot about our growth. He cares not just about our conversion but about our transformation too. He told parables about stewardship, seeds, soil, and the surrendered life. He never spoke of faith as a one-time event but rather a way of life, walking intimately with Him, learning what it means to follow Him.

In chapter 15 of Luke's gospel, we read the story about the prodigal son who ruthlessly demanded his inheritance before his father even died. He had oats to sow and didn't care who he hurt. But when he came to the end of himself, he made his way back home. Before he even had the chance to explain himself, his father wrapped him in a warm embrace and declared there'd be a homecoming party.

Meanwhile, the older brother was hard at work in the fields. When he returned home he heard music and dancing in the house and learned about the reason for the party. The brother was beside himself. He refused to go into the place, so his father went outside to meet with him. The son lamented (and I paraphrase), "I've slaved all these years for you and never once refused to do what you asked of me. And in all that time, you never once gave me a young goat for a feast with my friends. Yet when this son of yours returns home after squandering your money, you celebrate!"

The father looked at his son and said, "Look, dear son, you have always stayed by me, and everything I have is yours. We had to celebrate this happy day. For your brother was dead and has come back to life. He was lost, but now he is found!"[2]

There's more than one way to wander and more than one way to squander all God has made available to us. The younger son thought he could take his father's blessings and make his own way, apart from having a relationship with his father. The older son assumed that because he hadn't rebelled he was in right relationship with his father. He thought he understood what it meant to be a beloved son. But his attitude revealed otherwise.

When we walk intimately with the Father and grow to know Him more and more, His influence purges us from presumption and entitlement. We realize that any gift from His hand pales in comparison to the treasure of knowing His heart. Walking in God's presence, getting to know His heart, is what changes us from the inside out.

These two immature sons—amid their blind spots and hang-ups—were met by a merciful father intent on a relationship with them.

When both rebels and pharisees encounter the living God and follow Him on His terms, we finally see ourselves as we really are. When we humble ourselves and turn to God, we enjoy rich fellowship with a loving Father who knows our hearts and knows what we need. And amazingly, after a God-encounter, former pharisees and rebels sometimes even find fellowship with each other, just as God always designed it to be. Our capacity for self-deception is high (we're quick to see others' flaws but not so quick to discern our own). But God's mercy and passionate pursuit of us is greater still.

It's a stunning paradox to consider that while God is well aware of our weaknesses, immaturities, and unhealed areas, He simultaneously *embraces us and sees us* as holy priests, beloved children, and altogether righteous. All because of what Jesus won for us.

First Peter 2 tells us,

> And you are living stones that God is building into his spiritual temple. What's more, you are his holy priests. Through the mediation of Jesus Christ, you offer spiritual sacrifices that please God. . . . You are a chosen people. You are royal priests, a holy nation, God's very own possession. As a result, you can show others the goodness of God, for he called you out of the darkness into his wonderful light. "Once you had no identity as a people; now you are God's people. Once you received no mercy; now you have received God's mercy."[3]

Before Jesus we had no identity, but now we're royalty. Before Jesus we were stuck in our sin, but now we're forgiven and free. Our sin no longer has the legal right to eternally condemn us.

Imagine! Before Jesus we were powerless to change, but now we have the very power of the risen Lord alive and at work within us. The gravity of sin is no match for the resurrection capacity mightily at work within us!

Before Jesus, the promises of God were out of reach, and now they're all yes and amen! Before Jesus we faced a Christless eternity. Now we can look forward with holy anticipation because He's preparing a place for us, a banquet, and an eternity that will take our breath away. We can look forward to living forever with our Savior and King, and no one can take our inheritance away from us.

In the meantime, we *grow* in the grace of God and in our knowledge of Him. And we stay humbly teachable every step of the way. Here are just a few passages from Scripture that speak to our charge to grow as we go:

> So let us stop going over the basic teachings about Christ again and again. Let us go on instead and become mature in our understanding. Surely we don't need to start again with the fundamental importance of repenting from evil deeds and placing our faith in God.[4]

> The seeds that fell among the thorns represent those who hear the message, but all too quickly the message is crowded out by the cares and riches and pleasures of this life. And so they never grow into maturity. And the seeds that fell on the good soil represent honest, good-hearted people who hear God's word, cling to it, and patiently produce a huge harvest.[5]

> And now, just as you accepted Christ Jesus as your Lord, you must continue to follow him. Let your roots grow down into

him, and let your lives be built on him. Then your faith will grow strong in the truth you were taught, and you will over-flow with thankfulness.[6]

We get to be a work in progress without the condemnation. We live at the pace of grace. God doesn't hurry us through our hurts, but He doesn't leave us in them either. He's always invit-ing us upward and onward to the better things He has for us. Maturity doesn't happen overnight or even over time without our cooperation.

You've heard the phrase "Some people never change," and while that can appear true in certain situations, what's truer still is that we're constantly changing. We're either becoming more embedded with the lies that hold us captive, or with God's help and cooperation, we're breaking free and moving on to new levels of wholeness, freedom, and fruitfulness.

Even Jesus—the Son of God, the second person of the Trinity—*grew*, advanced, and moved forward during His days on earth. As Luke 2:52 says, "Jesus grew in wisdom and in stature and in favor with God and all the people."

Miracles in the Making

Years ago, one of my sons worked with a person who was demeaning, nitpicky, and didn't know anything about kindness, encouragement, or vision. Every day was a drudgery, and my son lost heart over time. The light went out of his eyes. He prayed. He forgave. He started each new day again, only to find himself stuck in an impossible situation.

One day he lamented to me, "I can't keep going like this, Mom. I need something to change." My heart broke for him. I prayed passionately and encouraged him as best I could, but wisdom from one of my other sons set his heart right. He grabbed his brother by the shoulders and said, "Look, bro, God is all around you! You're a walking miracle!"

"What do you mean I'm a walking miracle?"

His brother continued, "You're working in an impossible situation, yet every night you faithfully go home to your wife; you kiss her and tell her you love her. That's a miracle. You're still hilariously funny and kind and insightful. You've not let this bitter boss destroy you. Yes, this is hard, but what if God is growing strength and perseverance in you? Maybe you'll need this fortitude in the future."

His word proved right. My son leaned in, looked for the good amid all the bad, and found his soul encouraged. He determined to look for growth and celebrate it. He learned not to take insults from his boss so personally, even though she meant them that way. He somehow found his joy. And then, one day, God opened the door for him to move on to a better place. My pastor always used to say that you're not free to go until you're free to stay. The various storms in my son's life have sent his roots down deep. I look at him now as an oak of righteousness.

Most of us attribute the

> Growth isn't just about biding our time through difficult seasons. It's about learning to cast our cares more quickly upon the One who cares for us. It's about learning how to practice God's presence in the everyday grind of life.

significant growth in our life to the things we've suffered, the ways we've failed, or the seasons we had to endure. But growth isn't just about biding our time through difficult seasons. It's about learning to cast our cares more quickly upon the One who cares for us. It's about learning how to practice God's presence in the everyday grind of life. It's about learning to rest, laugh, and play while we wait for our breakthrough. It's about counting life's blessings when the burdens feel especially heavy. It's about coming under Jesus' light and easy yoke and trusting Him to do the heavy lifting.

John Eldredge writes,

> If you want to become a wholehearted person, you must reach the point where happily, lovingly, you give absolutely everything over to God. You make Jesus your everything, your all-in-all. Not only is this the fulfillment of your heart's created destiny, it is the source of all recovery and resilience. Nothing can be taken from you because you've already surrendered everything.[7]

Scripture says that daily the heavens pour forth speech. God moves night and day on behalf of His people. He never sleeps. He works while we rest. And yet there seem to be certain seasons of dispensation when God moves on a broader scale, in tangible, noticeable ways in different regions of the world or communities of faith.

With that in mind, consider the importance of preparing your heart and life for the next great outpouring. How do we prepare, you ask? We till the soil. We uproot the weeds. We plant new seeds. *We prepare for growth.*

Let's look at Hebrews 6:7–8:

> When the ground soaks up the falling rain and bears a good
> crop for the farmer, it has God's blessing. But if a field bears
> thorns and thistles, it is useless. The farmer will soon con-
> demn that field and burn it.

Consider your heart and life a field. The rain is coming,
friend. God hears the cries of His people. When the rain falls on
a prepared field, it bears a good crop and receives God's blessing.
The seeds we sow in ready soil will always produce a harvest.
Heavy rain creates a big mess when a field of thickets, thorns, and
stones soaks it up. Let's look at the rest of this passage:

> Dear friends, even though we are talking this way, we really
> don't believe it applies to you. We are confident that you are
> meant for better things, things that come with salvation.
> For God is not unjust. He will not forget how hard you have
> worked for him and how you have shown your love to him by
> caring for other believers, as you still do. Our great desire is
> that you will keep on loving others as long as life lasts, in order
> to make certain that what you hope for will come true. Then
> you will not become spiritually dull and indifferent. Instead,
> you will follow the example of those who are going to inherit
> God's promises because of their faith and endurance.[8]

We're meant for better things than what we've known thus
far. Better things that come with salvation. God sees you working your land. He sees you on your hands and knees, pulling
up weeds of resentment and unforgiveness because they don't

belong in you. He wants to grow you into freedom, wholeness, and fruitfulness more than you want these things for yourself. Jesus Himself said that we're appointed to bear fruit that outlasts us, and it's to our Father's great glory that it be so in our lives.[9] He honors your diligence in stewarding your life.

God sees you tossing out the stones and boulders that have hindered you for far too long. He sees how you till the soil with tenderness and sow seeds of kindness, goodness, love, and obedience into your field, and into others' fields too.

God hasn't missed a thing. He notices how you love Him and care for others. He loves watching you grow, and He will surely reward your faith. In due time, you will see a harvest. Don't give up.

For the Lord is the Spirit, and wherever the Spirit of the Lord is, there is freedom. So all of us who have had that veil removed can see and reflect the glory of the Lord. And the Lord—who is the Spirit—makes us more and more like him as we are changed into his glorious image.

2 CORINTHIANS 3:17–18

Reflect

1. Read Jeremiah 17:6–8 and write a paraphrased, personalized version of this passage.
2. Where in your life do you see growth? And how about barrenness? Write down your thoughts.
3. Read Psalm 92:10–15 along with this study note from the NLT *Life Application Study Bible*:

   Palm trees are known for their long life. To flourish like palm trees means to stand tall and to live long. The cedars of Lebanon grew to 120 feet in height and up to 30 feet in circumference; thus, they were solid, strong, and immovable. The writer saw believers as upright, strong, and unmoved by the winds of circumstance. Those who place their faith firmly in God can have this strength and vitality.[10]
4. How has God built strength into your character? How has He taught you to persevere? To what life experiences do you owe the most significant growth?

Pray

Precious Father, You are the Gardener, Your Son is the Vine, and all my life flows from my connection to You. I want to be like a tree planted by streams of water. I want to be so firmly planted in You that seasons of drought have no impact on me. My leaves will stay green, and I will continually bear fruit.[11] You loved me and rescued me before I even knew I needed saving. You drew me to Yourself by

Your Spirit, and now I'm alive in You! What a wonder it is to belong to You. And it pleases You to make me strong. Give me a vision for how You want me to grow. Help me to rightly interpret my battles and conflicts; help me to see them as the fertile soil for You to do something stunningly new in me. I am Yours, and You are mine. Your banner over me is love. I will trust in Your love, rest in Your care, and count on You to grow Your likeness in me. I'm safe with You. I love You, Lord. Amen.

Respond

Purchase a small indoor garden (which can be as simple as a small sampling of herbs). Plant the seeds and pray for God's blessing. Notice the waiting period and praise God for the life that bursts forth underground before your eyes ever see it. Celebrate the sprout that breaks through the soil. Stand in awe of God. He gives life and breath to every living thing[12] (Acts 17:24–25).

Ask God to highlight growth all around you. May He open your eyes to see subtle shifts in character, attitude, and openness to the things of God. Each time you notice growth, look up and thank your God.

Ponder His Presence

If God Can Intervene, Why Doesn't He?

Why does God heal one and not the other? Why do some seem to skate through life while others suffer one hardship after another? Why do we enjoy sunny days at the park and lunch out with friends while perpetrators abuse little boys and girls multiple times a day in a rape-for-profit crime ring? Evil men make despicable choices, and the most vulnerable suffer. Why?

It's almost too much to ponder, isn't it? These questions have kept me up at night. I don't know the full answers to these mysteries, but here's what I do know: God loves us so much, He refused to take control of our wills. He gave us the free will to love Him or not; to choose Him or not. To be kind or cruel. Left to ourselves and our choices, we were destined for destruction, so He sent His Son to save us. God made a way for us not to destroy ourselves but to be made new by offering us new life in Him.

When Jesus told His disciples He needed to leave, He said, "It is best for you that I go."[1] What? How is it better for us if our miracle-working Savior departs from the earth? It's better because He would send His Holy Spirit to empower the life of every believer on the planet. Though Jesus was God, He operated within the bounds of His humanity. He could only be in one place at a time. But now? Millions of Christians are mobilized throughout the earth.

It was Christians who started schools and universities. Christians who initiated ministries to the poor. Christians who stepped in to stop human traffickers. And Christians who take medical mission trips every year to help those with no hope. This is not to say that nonbelievers do no humanitarian work. But it does show that breathtaking miracles are happening all around the globe because Christians are mobilized, on mission, by the power of the Holy Spirit.

You are the God who performs miracles, you display your power among the peoples.

PSALM 77:14 (NIV)

God isn't sitting up in heaven twiddling His thumbs while Satan gets away with murder down here. Picture our mighty God pointing to His people and mobilizing warring angels on our behalf. Things are happening in the spiritual realm and on earth because God is busy and active in the hearts of His people. He's performing wonders too great to imagine because of our prayers.

We can blame God all day for the world's suffering, but it's not His fault. It's the work of our Enemy. And God has equipped *us*, appointed *us*, and anointed *us* for service.

When it comes to our own personal suffering, I have a few thoughts on the matter. People have said things to me like, "You're a leader at your level, and you're still not healed? Where's your faith?" *Ouch.* I've contended for the promises of God. He has worked wonders in my life. But if there's one thing I've learned, it's this: there's no formula for getting God to do what we want Him to do. Yes, our faith matters. But there's also a mystery to God's ways.

It's not enough to throw your hands in the air and leave your healing and wholeness to chance. Your faith matters, and it pleases God. I'm different because of the ways I've engaged my faith and believed God for all He's promised me. But it's unkind to blame the sick for their suffering and to assume they somehow missed a step.

When John the Baptist was imprisoned and away from the action, he started to question whether Jesus was who He said He was. That John had doubts should encourage you. Jesus responded to John's questions by telling him that miracles are still happening even if he's not a witness to them. Then Jesus said, "Blessed is he who is not offended because of Me."[2]

I think that's our work in this hour. To believe that He's still a miracle-working God, even if our circumstances hinder us from witnessing those miracles in the moment. And to keep our hearts clean, pure, and unoffended by God. He's not the reason we suffer. And He promises to redeem every heartache, every tear, and every sorrow we've ever faced. He's a good, good God.

Prayer

Father, help me to trust Your will when it's hard for me to trust Your ways. I know You are good. I know You don't miss a thing. Help me to hold fast to faith, hope, and love, knowing one day You'll make all things right again. I love You, Lord. Amen.

nine

God Has Called You

For Such a Time As This

*Every single person on the planet today is on a spiritual journey.
Each one of us is either failing or sailing, walking by faith or stuck
in place, surviving or thriving. If you feel unable to move beyond
your plow, to accept the mantle of promotion God has for you,
then perhaps it is time to reconsider your focus. Are you looking
down when you should be looking up?*

SAMUEL RODRIGUEZ

In my late teens, I decided to take up running. One day I ran
farther than my body appreciated. I didn't stop to walk; I was
determined to finish the race (even though it wasn't actually a
race). I turned the corner into my neighborhood, heaving and
gasping for air. I was so exhausted that I couldn't run a straight
line. I zigged left, veered right, tripped over myself, caught my
footing, and zigged left again. My arms flailed this way and that.

My feet hurt, which caused my legs to jerk out from under me with every step. I'm not sure why I didn't put myself out of my misery and just slow down to a walk.

My neighbor peeked her head out her front door and asked, "Everything okay, Susie?" I looked surprised and said, "Yeah. Why do you ask?" She bit her bottom lip, forced a smile, gave me a nod, and closed the door. Then it occurred to me why she wondered about me. I ran like an injured antelope. For a person who cared too deeply about what people thought of me at that stage of life, I sure didn't care quite enough that day. I still laugh when I think about that memory.

I soon learned about single-minded focus and purposeful steps. We waste all kinds of energy with sideways movements that don't propel us forward. After receiving some coaching from those who understood the sport's technical side, I soon stream-lined my efforts and learned to run with efficiency and grace. I ran seven miles a day for years. Eventually, Lyme wrecked my joints, so I took up cycling. Running prepared me for biking. Even so, I had new things to learn about maximizing my efforts on the bike.

Your past experiences and battles have prepared you for where you stand now. Though you've had to learn new skills to navigate new terrains, God leads and transforms you as you go. When God moves you on to the next place He has for you, you may temporarily feel displaced, out of sorts, and out of shape. But in due time, you'll hit your stride and know how to run your race with purpose in every step. Don't be afraid to start again. Don't worry if you feel ill-equipped or out of place. God will establish your steps. But He wants you in the race.

Consider Paul. He was once a Pharisee who grew up in the home of a Pharisee. I suppose you could say he'd mastered pharisaism. Look how he described himself:

> I am a Jew, born in Tarsus, a city in Cilicia, and I was brought up and educated here in Jerusalem under Gamaliel. As his student, I was carefully trained in our Jewish laws and customs. I became very zealous to honor God in everything I did, just like all of you today. And I persecuted the followers of the Way, hounding some to death, arresting both men and women and throwing them in prison. The high priest and the whole council of elders can testify that this is so. For I received letters from them to our Jewish brothers in Damascus, authorizing me to bring the followers of the Way from there to Jerusalem, in chains, to be punished.[1]

Christians considered Paul a terrorist because he ruthlessly oppressed and persecuted their families and communities. Picture husbands and wives clinging to one another, crying out for help as Paul dragged them from their homes, separated them, and put them in prison. He spit at their feet and walked away with the keys. No mercy. No compassion. Only self-righteousness. He lived with purpose, alright.

Paul was on a mission to destroy Christians and demolish the church—a cause he thought was noble and righteous. But then one day, Jesus drew near. The Lord broke through Paul's legalistic fog and revealed His power and glory. Paul was forever changed; thus, the world was never the same. Here's how Paul described what happened:

As I was on the road, approaching Damascus about noon, a very bright light from heaven suddenly shone down around me. I fell to the ground and heard a voice saying to me, "Saul, Saul, why are you persecuting me?"

"Who are you, lord?" I asked.

And the voice replied, "I am Jesus the Nazarene, the one you are persecuting." The people with me saw the light but didn't understand the voice speaking to me.

I asked, "What should I do, Lord?"

And the Lord told me, "Get up and go into Damascus, and there you will be told everything you are to do."[2]

Try to imagine that moment. Jesus appeared years after His resurrection. A bright light shone. God's voice thundered. Paul dropped to his knees, covered his eyes, and cried out for answers.

God's presence changes everything. The power and presence of our risen Lord invaded Paul's life, opening his eyes to the reality of his Savior and saving him from destruction. God intercepted Paul on the road that day for the sake of millions who would one day be instructed by this mighty man of faith. God's glory blinded Paul's earthly eyes and opened his spiritual eyes.

The former Saul, now called Paul, was instantly humbled and profoundly awakened to the truth about who God is. He went from being an expert Pharisee to a baby believer in only a matter of days. Paul had a lot to learn about being a follower of the Way. But the Lord put people in Paul's path to help him, and the Holy Spirit within to guide him. In time, Paul would become one of the greatest missionaries in Christian history.

Paul was bold, brave, courageous, and full of conviction. He didn't fear men; he feared God. He didn't waste time; he redeemed the time he was given. Paul kept his eyes heavenward so that his days on earth would count for eternity. Paul suffered much for being a Christ-follower. And God—through Paul—gave us some of the most remarkable books of the Bible.

Paul wrote a letter to believers in the Corinthian church to help them navigate their faith in a corrupt culture. Many Gentile believers lived there amid idolatry, immorality, and decadence. Paul urged God's people not to get distracted but to stay the course, eyes fixed and hearts set on eternity. His words ring true for us today.

> Do you not know that in a race all the runners run [their very best to win], but only one receives the prize? Run [your race] in such a way that you may seize the prize and make it yours! Now every athlete who [goes into training and] competes in the games is disciplined and exercises self-control in all things. They do it to win a crown that withers, but we [do it to receive] an imperishable [crown that cannot wither]. Therefore I do not run without a definite goal; I do not flail around like one beating the air [just shadow boxing]. But [like a boxer] I strictly discipline my body and make it my slave, so that, after I have preached [the gospel] to others, I myself will not somehow be disqualified [as unfit for service].[3]

Athletes train for a crown that withers. Christians train for a crown that lasts forever. We run for a much greater prize than a gold medal. Eternity awaits us. How we live here directly impacts how we live there, in heaven, with Jesus, forever. Our choices matter. Our calling matters. Whether or not we engage with the things of God matters deeply.

We Serve a Good King

As Christians, God calls us to steward our moments and days because we're part of another kingdom. We serve a good King who promises to redeem every act prompted by our faith. He never forces compliance, but He rewards obedience. He never shames us for our weakness; He shines brightly through the lowly places in our lives. He never bullies us into surrender, but He does lovingly dare us to trust Him. And when we do, life springs forth.

As people of the kingdom, we've been bought with a price.[4] We're no longer our own. God has every right to force us into service, but instead He woos us into intimacy. He doesn't call us slaves; He calls us friends. He opens our eyes to the spiritual dimension. He confides in us with insight that's otherworldly. He speaks life to us through His living Word. He breathes life in us through His Holy Spirit. And He equips us to navigate life behind enemy lines until He comes again.

We're part of something so much greater than ourselves. While we were yet sinners, Christ died for us. He made a way where there was no way. He prepared our calling before we ever knew we needed one. He determined our redemption long before we were ever born. He established us in His goodness and mercy and sustains us through His power and grace. We were orphans. And now we're heirs. We partner with the Almighty to fulfill His purposes on the earth. And when He returns, He'll gladly display us before a watching world, claiming us as His prized possessions. Could we possibly be more blessed?

Why would we waste our time on indulgences that distract and pursuits that bear no fruit? Now is the time to put it all on the table, ask God for direction, and give Him permission to rearrange our lives for our good and His glory. Anything He awakens within us will change us for the better. We're most alive when we're in the center of His will.

C.S. Lewis wrote,

> It would seem that Our Lord finds our desires not too strong, but too weak. We are half-hearted creatures, fooling about with drink and sex and ambition when infinite joy is offered us, like an ignorant child who wants to go on making mud pies in a slum because he cannot imagine what is meant by the offer of a holiday at the sea. We are far too easily pleased.[5]

Do you want to come alive? Ask God to invade your life with His powerful light. Ask Him to show you what you can't see and teach you what you don't know. Scroll through your contacts on your phone and prayerfully consider who you might ask over for dinner. Lean in and listen to their stories. Care for their needs. Pray for them before they leave.

Gather a few faith-filled friends and pray purposefully about the burdens of your heart. Pray God's Word. Remind your soul how great God is!

Sow some faith seeds into a ministry that God has highlighted. Imagine the poor fed, the lost found, and the church being mobilized all because you gave. Add faith to your deeds. Picture life bursting forth from the seeds you planted in the kingdom.

Ask God to use you in ways above and beyond your abilities and capacity. Be willing to move out of your comfort zone. Trade saving face for saving grace. Be a learner. Get ready to be the newbie in the group. Your identity is never up for grabs. So go where He sends you.

Then just do the next thing He tells you to do. And do it with your faith engaged, your ears wide open, and your eyes fixed on Him. You become spiritually agile, strong, and steadfast when you move with Him. He's on the move on the earth today.

> **We serve the God of the breakthrough! God rescues us from our enemies, heals our hurts, and trains us for battle. He invites us to partner with Him on earth. He equips us to carry out our call. And He rewards us for trusting Him to do the impossible in and through us.**

We serve the God of the breakthrough! Our God is not only a good King but also a fierce Warrior and a loving Physician. God rescues us from our enemies, heals our hurts, and trains us for battle. He invites us to partner with Him on earth. He equips us to carry out our call. And He rewards us for trusting Him to do the impossible in and through us.

As followers of Jesus, we *practice* self-control, persistence, and patience while many in the world indulge, give up, and blow up. We don't defy God. We rely on God. We don't live like there's no tomorrow because we know many tomorrows await us. And our efforts and attitudes today have eternal implications for tomorrow. When we love Jesus, enjoy His presence, and follow His lead, His light shines brightly in our hearts, displacing the darkness around us.

In 2 Corinthians 4:6–7, the apostle Paul explained it like this:

For God, who said, "Let there be light in the darkness," has made this light shine in our hearts so we could know the glory of God that is seen in the face of Jesus Christ.

We now have this light shining in our hearts, but we ourselves are like fragile clay jars containing this great treasure. This makes it clear that our great power is from God, not from ourselves.

We inspire others to fill their space and run their race when we live with purpose and passion. Sometimes we surprise ourselves, run farther than we thought possible, and accomplish more than we'd hoped. Sometimes our offering seems puny, yet the outcome is profound. We must never overestimate our strengths nor underestimate what God can do with our sincere offerings. Even a cup of cold water in His name gets noticed in heaven.

Sometimes we get tired and want to quit. Sometimes we run like an injured antelope. Sometimes we get it wrong. Sometimes we fall and fumble the ball.

God doesn't want perfect. He wants progress. If we're willing to follow, the Holy Spirit will lead, set the pace, and determine our steps. And we will be changed along the way.

We live in a day of acceleration. Though there are still sixty seconds in every minute, more is happening every minute in our culture than some have seen in their lifetime. Our past battle strategies may not work for us in the present. This is no time for disengaged, autopilot Christianity, nor is it time to fight people over issues that the Enemy is behind. Some are numbing out while others are boiling over.

But as people of God, we love people and keep our hope in

God. We wage war in the spiritual realm where our battles are fought and won. As 2 Corinthians 10:3–5 reminds us,

> We are human, but we don't wage war as humans do. We use God's mighty weapons, not worldly weapons, to knock down the strongholds of human reasoning and to destroy false arguments. We destroy every proud obstacle that keeps people from knowing God. We capture their rebellious thoughts and teach them to obey Christ.

How Do We Walk Out Our Call?

In a practical sense, how do we walk out our call in these chaotic, distracting times? Though calling looks different on all of us, given our gifts, passions, and seasons of life, these common threads will bind us together in Christ as we eagerly wait for His return.

Walk Intimately with God

First and foremost, we put a high priority on our moment-by-moment walk with God. We treasure His Word, listen for His voice, and do what He says. May our intimate relationship with the Father, Son, and Holy Spirit be the most important thing about our lives. May we grow to enjoy and count on God's presence more than anything else.

Stay in Fellowship with Godly Friends

Second, we discern whom God has appointed us to walk closely with in this season in the kingdom. As the times change and culture shifts, so may our inner circle of friends. May we find like-minded believers who pray passionately, live purposefully, and earnestly desire more of God's influence in our lives.

Pray for and Love the Lost

Third, we daily consider those who don't know Jesus. He came to seek and save the lost,[6] and He is right now reaching the world through His friends. When you give to the poor, you lend to the Lord, and He will repay you.[7] When you share about the hope of Jesus with another, you plant seeds. When you help fund missionary journeys, you make a global kingdom impact. Sometimes we become so self-focused that we drift off mission. Though God cares deeply about our lives, He's delaying His return because He doesn't want *any* to perish; He's waiting for many of His children to repent.[8] Every living Christian is called to care about the lost. May the Lord awaken our hearts to love, concern, and compassion for those who would absolutely love Jesus if only they knew Him.

Pray Like You Mean It

Fourth, we become audacious praying people who dare to stand on God's promises and believe Him for great things. When we pray with others in agreement with God and specifically for the things He has promised, answers come, mountains move, and miracles burst onto the scene. Our world needs more miracles.

Grow in Generosity

Fifth, if we haven't already, we grow in the grace of giving. Generosity is prominent in God's character and beautifully expressed through generous Christians. Based on stats alone, most Christians still live with a scarcity mindset. Imagine what would happen if we *all* awakened to the divinely generous nature of God! Churches and ministries would be fully funded, the poor fed, and those experiencing homelessness would find a home. And daily, we'd be reminded that God supplies all our needs according to His riches, not ours.[9] May we become such generous seed-sowers that the world repeatedly rejoices over the goodness of God.

Now he who supplies seed to the sower and bread for food will also supply and increase your store of seed and will enlarge the harvest of your righteousness. You will be enriched in every way so that you can be generous on every occasion, and through us your generosity will result in thanksgiving to God.

2 CORINTHIANS 9:10–11 (NIV)

God Is Moving His People to New Places

Have you noticed? God is repositioning His saints. At every turn, I see God moving people out of lifelong jobs and into newly created positions. Pulling saints out of retirement and recommissioning them back into ministry. Moving one across the country to step into a role they never dreamed possible. Transitioning another into a place of leadership they never aspired to. Shifting one into a place of hidden intercession and another into a place of public advocacy. It's like a chess match. The devil is on the move, but God already has a plan, and His purposes *will* prevail. And we're part of that plan.

Consider others in Scripture who surely felt displaced when God called them from what they knew to a place that was at first unknown:

> The devil is on the move, but God already has a plan, and His purposes *will* prevail. And we're part of that plan.

- Abraham: Called to leave a land he knew to go to a place that was yet to be revealed.
- Joseph: Betrayed by family, hauled away by slave traders, but sent ahead by God for a divine purpose—to lead a nation through seasons of feast and famine.
- Ruth: Left her homeland to follow a God she could not see to a place she didn't know to be grafted into the lineage of Christ.
- Moses: Called out of hiding to face his fears and lead God's chosen people out of captivity.
- Esther: Called away from her safe, simple home and into a palace where God used her to rescue His chosen people.
- Daniel: Taken captive and snatched from his homeland, forced to serve a king, and used to bring glory to the One true King of the ages.

These are just a few scriptural examples of how God uses

earthly events to activate His eternal purposes. God calls us not because He needs us; God calls us because every God-sized assignment reminds us how much we need Him. We encounter God, and He empowers us to serve Him. Not because He *trusts* us. He wisely equips and empowers us to accomplish that which He *entrusts to us*. The more we trust God, the more trustworthy we find Him. And the more we learn to trust Him *more than we trust ourselves*, the more He entrusts to us.[10]

If God calls you to walk through the valley, He'll prepare a table for you there. If He calls you to walk through the water, He'll reach out His hand and lift you up to walk on water with Him. If He calls you to something you feel grossly unqualified for, He will sustain you every step of the way. And you can feel sure you heard Him correctly because He always does that with His children. He calls us because He's well able to qualify us and glorify Himself as we go.

Grow to Love God's Presence

Let's circle back to Paul's story for a moment. I once heard about a major news anchor who decided to trust Jesus for salvation. In zero to sixty seconds flat, Christians hopped on Facebook to tell her how and why she needed to change all her worldly opinions into biblical ones. I don't know what happened to her or her faith journey, but I can tell you that this scenario deeply grieved my heart. This woman may have had a major national platform, but she was still a baby Christian. To expect her to step into a full-blown, mature faith is unfair, and to pressure her to change is legalistic.

After a gospel presentation, when I have the honor to pray with those who decide to trust Jesus for salvation, I often close with a statement like this: "So grateful to have you in the family of God. I encourage you to read your Bible regularly, prayerfully. Get into a Bible-believing church. Get to know other Christians and walk closely with them. However, if you encounter a seemingly 'seasoned' Christian who looks down her nose at you and tells you how good Christians ought to act, and you feel no love or compassion coming from her . . . *run*. External pressure does not change a heart. Love does.

"When you said yes to Jesus, His Spirit took up residence in your soul. He's alive in you! Now when you say something or do something contrary to His will, you may feel that inner wince that tells you that God wants you to make a different choice. A more redemptive one. Over time, as you respond to the nudges of the Spirit within you, your tastes will change. You will change. But it's God mightily at work within you. It's real. It's beautiful. And it's sustainable. Grow to love His presence in your life and you'll continue to grow for the rest of your life."

I share this because I believe we're about to come into a great awakening followed by an unprecedented harvest. I think we may see some high-profile, highly unlikely "Sauls" who encounter Jesus in unbelievably life-changing ways. Maybe they'll be some of the most radical opponents of the faith who become radical advocates for the kingdom. They'll have rough edges. They won't come ready-made. But then again, neither did we. Can we handle it if God raises up some of the most unlikely souls to wake up the church and call in lost souls?

Things are about to get wild, I believe. And if we're living with a fossilized faith and long for the old days, we're going to

> *The servants who are ready and waiting for his return will be rewarded. I tell you the truth, he himself will seat them, put on an apron, and serve them as they sit and eat!*
>
> LUKE 12:37

miss the move of God in our days. We can't cling to our once-treasured role at the church or our job that gives us a certain status. God is moving things around so He can turn things around. He gets the say, so He can have His way.

If we're willing to engage with Him, walk with Him, and trust Him with our whole hearts, we'll get to be a part of one of the most extraordinary moves of God this planet has ever seen.

Your purpose in this crucial time is to be much with God. To walk intimately with Him and enjoy His presence. To know His Word, recognize His voice, and do what He says. Quickly. Not later. Right now. And to ask Him to move mightily on the earth and do the impossible through you. God wants to use you in ways that will take your breath away. You were appointed to be alive, breathing, and serving God for such a time.

Reflect

1. Read Ephesians 2:10 and write a personalized, paraphrased version of this passage.
2. Based on this passage and Romans 8:28, here's what's

true: You are a beautiful, masterful work of art, created by God's hand. He's called you to do good work for His glory. He promises to take every aspect of your story—*all things*—and work them together for your good and His glory because you're called and living according to *His purpose*, not yours. As you sit with these beautiful truths for a bit, ask the Lord to uncover any lingering insecurity or lack of confidence. Ask Him to show you what's at the root of these feelings. Write down your thoughts.

3. Is there a story from Scripture that you return to time and time again? For example, Ruth, Joseph, or Deborah? If so, reread the story, ask God to highlight what He wants you to see, and write down your thoughts. And write down the parts that God highlights for you. If no story comes, consider reading Esther's story prayerfully.

4. If God were to move mightily in your day and ask you to step out of your comfort zone, what might that look like?

Pray

High King of Heaven, I worship You! I give You thanks and praise. You transferred me from the kingdom of darkness and brought me into the kingdom of light. You've made me an heir! I have an eternal inheritance waiting for me because of Jesus. Forgive me for the times I forget who I am and why I'm here. Lord, help me discern the times and know what to do. Help me identify the distractions that pull me away from You. I want to run this race to win. Overwhelm me with a sense of Your presence, love, and purpose for me. Give me faith to believe You for miracles. Help me see those You've given me to serve, love, and assist. Bless me with prayer warrior friends who call me higher and encourage me to go deeper with You. I'm done messing around with lesser things. I want to live ready for Your soon return. I want to play a part in the coming kingdom. Here I am, Lord. Use me. Send me. Awaken me! Amen.

Respond

Light a candle. Open your Bible. Grab your journal. And ponder the idea of another Great Awakening. Ask the Lord to show you how He'd want to use you. His answer might surprise you. He may invite you to join Him in ways you never imagined.

Clear out the clutter and create a space where you can sit with God. Rehearse Ephesians 2:10 and Romans 8:28 and remind your soul about the truths in these passages. Smile at the thought that you're in the faithful hands of a great God.

Ponder His Presence

What Does It Mean to Fix Our Eyes on What We Cannot See?

I sat on my comfy chair with my Bible in my lap and considered the verse I'd just read on the page. I love to look out the window while I'm pondering Scripture. I see the sky as one of God's great works of art, which changes daily. As I thought through the passage I'd just read, I looked out the window, hoping for a fresh revelation.

My mind wandered to window washing and other big chores piling up around me. I noticed bird droppings on the outside of the window, too high for me to reach with a ladder and wipe clean. My eyes zeroed in on the bird poo, and I completely forgot about the verse I'd just read.

Then I heard the whisper. *Look above it. Look past it.* I got up from my chair, walked to the window to look at the beautiful sky better, and found my focus again. A bird dropping is hardly anything to fret about, but it reminded me of all the times I've set my gaze on things intended to distract me from the best of what God has for me.

When we zero in on what's in front of us, we miss so much of what God has promised us. The apostle Paul said,

> For our present troubles are small and won't last very long. Yet they produce for us a glory that vastly outweighs them and will last forever! So we don't look at the troubles we can see now; rather, we fix our gaze on things that cannot be seen. For the things we see now will soon be gone, but the things we cannot see will last forever.[1]

It sounds like an oxymoron to fix our eyes on what we cannot see. But if we scoot a little closer, we'll find powerful wisdom in this passage. The phrase "fix our gaze" means to observe, contemplate, mark, and direct one's attention to.[2]

Life is full of moments that distract us with temporary issues that hold little eternal value. Scripture challenges us not to ignore what's happening in our world but to hold it up to the lens of eternity. To give special attention to that which is eternal. To continually observe spiritual truths and extract the priceless from the worthless. To intentionally mark our gaze. To live with the end in mind.

Sometimes we set our eyes so firmly on something that bothers us or something we lack that we miss the bounty of heaven right in our midst. God wants the eyes of our hearts to open wide! Look at Paul's prayer in his letter to the Ephesians:

> I keep asking that the God of our Lord Jesus Christ, the glorious Father, may give you the Spirit of wisdom and revelation, so that you may know him better. I pray that the eyes of your heart may be enlightened in order that you may know

the hope to which he has called you, the riches of his glorious inheritance in his holy people, and his incomparably great power for us who believe. That power is the same as the mighty strength he exerted when he raised Christ from the dead and seated him at his right hand in the heavenly realms, far above all rule and authority, power and dominion, and every name that is invoked, not only in the present age but also in the one to come.[3]

Imagine living with such focus and intention that you navigate life with a purposeful gaze. The Enemy continually throws distractions your way, but you wisely stay on mission; you keep directing your attention toward the things of God; you constantly contemplate the truths about eternity. You learn to live with holy expectancy.

Prayer

Jesus, open the eyes of my heart! Help me to be quick to notice when I'm losing focus—when I'm zeroing in on temporary problems and forgetting about Your eternal promises. May I live with eternity in mind. Amen.

ten

God Remembers; God Forgets

Live Loved; Live Free

God is not just a giver; he's also a forgiver. His grace is a persistent and pursuing one. . . . God has not chosen to love the lovable and the lovely. Rather, God's love is surprisingly indiscriminate, his favor roving and resting upon those who seem least deserving of it. God's grace is evidenced in his patient pursuit of the mucking-it-up.

JEN POLLOCK MICHEL

Several years ago, I ran into an old friend at a conference. I smiled when I saw her because I never knew her as a person of faith. But we had some things in common and enjoyed one another's company. I just loved her. We found a cozy place to sit, leaned in, and caught up on life. Her daughter's new Christian faith had inspired a spiritual hunger in my friend's heart. I was so grateful!

She looked me in the eyes and said, "Susie, do you remember years ago, when I was going through that terrible divorce?" I nodded, and she continued. "Do you remember when you gave me a hundred dollars for groceries? I'll never forget that moment. It meant the world to me."

> We're prone to rehearse the things God has decidedly forgotten. And we're just as apt to forget the things God has distinctly asked us to remember.

I sat back in my chair and said, "Hmm. I don't remember that at all. But do you want to know what I *do* remember? Every idiotic thing I've ever said, and what I was wearing when I said it!" We laughed. But my words were sadly true.

I don't think I'm alone when I say that we're prone to rehearse the things God has decidedly forgotten. And we're just as apt to forget the things God has distinctly asked us to remember.

His Presence Hovers; His Grace Covers

I've been camping out in the book of Genesis lately, overwhelmed by all the ways God's presence shows up in our stories even when we're unaware.

Though Abram's father worshiped idols, Abram had a heart for God. God told Abram to leave everything he knew and go to a land that God would reveal. He and his wife Sarai were barren, but God promised them a son and that their descendants would outnumber the stars. Sarai grew tired of waiting and thus accused God of something for which He was not guilty, which, in her mind, justified her solution.

> So Sarai said to Abram, "The LORD has prevented me from having children. Go and sleep with my servant. Perhaps I can have children through her." And Abram agreed with Sarai's proposal.[1]

God's timing—in every detail of our lives—is divinely wise and strategically timed. If it seems God is preventing us (at the moment) from having our heart's desires, it's often because He's preparing *us* to handle what He longs to entrust to us.

We must remember that our story is never just about our story. God continually works through countless events to transform us and establish His purposes on earth. I often say that He makes us wait because He's making us ready.

When we roll up our sleeves and insert ourselves where we don't belong, when we step into a story to force an outcome, we make messes where God was establishing order.

Despite our wandering ways, God is quick to forgive, offer grace, and move His purposes forward. He works all things together for our good and His glory.[2]

People ruin their lives by their own foolishness and then are angry at the LORD.

PROVERBS 19:3

It was Sarai's idea (not God's) that Abram should sleep with her servant *so she'd get pregnant and give them a son.* Yet when her idea backfired, she blamed her husband.

So Abram had sexual relations with Hagar, and she became pregnant. But when Hagar knew she was pregnant, she began to treat her mistress, Sarai, with contempt. Then Sarai said to Abram, "This is all your fault! I put my servant into your arms, but now that she's pregnant she treats me with contempt. The Lord will show who's wrong—you or me!"[3]

The Lord promised Abraham that he would be the father of many nations and that he'd become extremely fruitful.[4] Abraham bowed low to the ground but laughed on the inside. You can't blame him. Yes, he'd received a promise from the Lord, but he was a shriveled old man. Imagine him waking up slowly each morning to creaky joints and an achy back. It takes him forever to go to the bathroom, and he often forgets where he left his sandals. Not exactly prime conditions for a newborn.

How many promises have we abandoned because we deemed them out-of-date given our current season of life? But doesn't God do some of His best work in the eleventh hour? And before we judge Abraham for bowing low while laughing on the inside, how often do we go through life with a similar disconnect?

It's easy to sing worship songs while running through the grocery list in our heads. It's instinctive to speak Christian phrases without believing them in our hearts. Here's the thing: We disengage our hearts when we go through the motions. And when we disengage our hearts, we disconnect from our faith.

Faith Is Our Fuel

Faith is our fuel, and our actions give us traction. Nothing happens in the spiritual realm when we say one thing and believe another. We spin our wheels while the Enemy has his heyday in our lives.

But when we dig down deep and grab hold of the faith God imparted to us when we received His Son, and when we choose to *believe and therefore speak* words consistent with God's promises, the ground trembles beneath our feet. Mountains move; waters part. Hearts change. Heaven notices. And God's purposes are established in and all around us.

You may occasionally forget who you are, but God never does. You may remember your sins ad nauseum, but God never does. He remembers why He made you and how He made you. He knows what makes you laugh and what makes you cry. He knows what fires you up and what breaks your heart. He loves the masterpiece He crafted in you. He *remembers* His covenant to you. He *remembers* His promises. He knows where you're weak and gives you the strength you need when you need it most.

So even when your heart disconnects from your faith because you're weary in the waiting, God—in His grace—draws near to remind you what's true. God's nearness is always for our good.

When God draws near, His presence shines a light on our hearts. We suddenly see what we missed only moments ago. Conviction moves us to repentance. God's love draws us close. Jesus' blood washes away our sin. And heaven rewards our steps of obedience.

We are children of God. Safe and secure. Loved and called.

Our names are written in heaven. Our sins are at the bottom of the sea. God's willingness to forget and His power to remember make us the most blessed creatures of all creation.

God Remembers Our Faith, Not Our Sins

Back to the story. One day, Abraham was sitting outside his tent when he looked up and saw three men standing nearby. According to Scripture, the Lord and two angels visited Abraham. The angel told Abraham that Sarah (formerly Sarai) would have a son this time next year. Sarah listened from inside her tent and laughed to herself. The Lord asked Abraham why Sarah laughed, which she denied because she was afraid. It would be another fourteen years before Abraham and Sarah had a child of their own.

Though Abraham made plenty of mistakes, he had a heart for God. Yet it's easy to wonder if Sarah had a faith of her own or if she was along for the ride. Let's jump ahead to the New Testament to see what we can learn.

Faith shows the reality of what we hope for; it is the evidence of things we cannot see. Through their faith, the people in days of old earned a good reputation. . . .

It was by faith that Abraham obeyed when God called him to leave home and go to another land that God would give him as his inheritance. He went without knowing where he was going. And even when he reached the land God promised him, he lived there by faith—for he was like a foreigner, living in tents. And so did Isaac and Jacob, who inherited the same promise. Abraham was confidently looking forward to a city with eternal foundations, a city designed and built by God.

It was by faith that even Sarah was able to have a child, though she was barren and was too old. She believed that God would keep his promise. And so a whole nation came from this one man who was as good as dead—a nation with so many people that, like the stars in the sky and the sand on the seashore, there is no way to count them.[5]

A whole nation came from one man who was as good as dead. Try to wrap your brain around that one. The Bible says that through their faith, the people in the days of old *gained a good reputation*. Nowadays, these kinds of things would be reputation wreckers: Abraham lied about Sarah being his wife. He allowed his wife to boss him into sleeping with her servant. Sarah nagged him into disobedience and then blamed him for his actions.

And yet—and yet. The New Testament recognizes both Sarah and Abraham in the Hall of Faith. Sarah had seeds of faith in her own heart! God moved on that flicker of faith, and a whole nation was born through her union with her husband.

> Though history records some of Sarah's unflattering antics, *heaven remembers her faith.*

Though history records some of Sarah's unflattering antics, *heaven remembers her faith*. Don't rush by this point too fast. It oozes God's unfathomable, amazing grace. Abraham's willingness to trust God with his future changed the course of history.

What God Sees, What God Remembers

I shudder to think of all the embarrassing or sinful choices I've made in my past. If I think too long about it, my gut ties up in knots, and I feel all kinds of regret. But I'm under the blood of Jesus.

When God looks at me, He doesn't see what I see. When He considers my story, He doesn't remember what I remember. He remembers the day He transferred me out of the kingdom of darkness into the kingdom of His dear Son. He knows I belong to Him. He knows where I live. He remembers His promise to me.

Such profound love and amazing grace!

If you are in Christ, the same is true for you. Pause and consider this miraculous truth for a moment. The shame of your youth isn't even hiding in the corners of His mind. His thoughts about you outnumber the grains of sand on a seashore, and every thought toward you comes from a Father more committed to you than you are to yourself. If you could read His mind, you'd smile and finally believe that He genuinely, profoundly loves you.

Thanks to our Savior and King Jesus, when God looks at His children, He sees no spot or wrinkle or sinful memory that would mar our image before Him. God—our Father and righteous Judge—*sees us*, His children, as pure, forgiven, healed, and whole. He not only sees who we've become, He sees who we're becoming. Because of Jesus, God has put away the memory of our sins. The shame of our youth no longer gets a say in our future.

Our eternity is secure. Our robes are clean. Our hearts have been made new.

Refuse to allow your past to speak to you except to teach you. If the Lord calls you to revisit an old hurt, it's so He can heal you. If the Enemy bullies you into a past memory, it's so he can condemn you, which he has no legal right to do now that you're under the blood of the Lamb.

While we're busy giving airtime to the Enemy's accusations about our past, Jesus is earnestly preparing for our future. While the Enemy intently points out our flaws, Jesus purposefully advocates and intercedes for us. Right now, God is actively making notes of our offerings and obedience to Him.[6]

The devil knows that our sins can no longer condemn us, nor do they have the power to impact our eternal destination. He's just hoping we'll forget these powerful truths so he can continue to torment us in the present.

Anything he can do to steal our joy or dim our view of God, he'll do. Because the more we awaken to how secure we are in the Father's love, the more audaciously we'll dare to trust Him. And when we dare to trust Him and live by faith, that's when things change in the spiritual atmosphere. That's when heaven takes note.

If we could turn a deaf ear to the devil and bend an ear toward heaven, we'd be reminded afresh that Jesus is preparing a place for us right now. He's excitedly active, getting things ready for our grand homecoming.

Since we're God's children, filled with His Spirit, He delights in working wonders through us—often in ways that we dismiss because they seem small and insignificant. Amid our self-berating ways, we still pray, love, give, and serve because we genuinely love Jesus. What does God do with our sincere offerings of faith? He remembers. He rewards. He rewrites our history and plans for our glorious future in a way that only He can. Isn't the grace of God scandalously fabulous?

God wants you to live free, loved, and continually aware of

His amazing presence. He wants you to know that His will for you *is* your best-case scenario. He wants you to work as unto Him and rest because you trust Him. He wants you to entrust your past to Him, and your future too. He wants you to live with an ever-increasing awareness of His nearness. His presence makes all the difference in your life. And He's with you every step of the way. When you grow to know and love God intimately, you'll learn to trust Him with all the things you cannot—and were never meant to—control. His presence is your protection and provision.

Internal medicine physician and expert on rest Dr. Saundra Dalton-Smith writes:

> You are free to participate with God. Free to live, free to move, and free to be. No longer confined to overperforming and overachieving. Resting in the smallness and the greatness. . . . Possessing the boldness to fertilize where you desire abundant harvest. No longer pushing the limits demanding your way but participating in the delicate exchange between faith and action. Working from a place of being acknowledged, affirmed, and approved. This is work under grace. Work born from the rest of being intimately known and accepted.[7]

I don't want to be one of God's children who squanders my faith to the point that I barely escape the flames. I want to live all-in, on mission, full of faith, and abounding in love. I want to take Him at His word and trust Him for the things I cannot see. I want to live a life that God is thrilled to reward and establish because we're in sync and my heart beats in rhythm with His. I want my life to bear all the fruit God intended from before time.[8] I think you want that too.

We're called to live intimately in sync with Jesus, to be pliable in the Father's hand. To be faithful, humble, and teachable. And to remember what He remembers and forget what He's determined to forget.

God Generously Rescues

Let's go back to Abraham's story once more.

Abraham's nephew Lot grew wealthy under Abraham's wing. In due time, the flocks multiplied, the herdsmen began to bicker, and Abraham took the initiative to protect the relationship. He said (my paraphrase), "My dear nephew, we're family. Let's not allow anything to come between us. Our herds have grown exponentially, and it's clear we each need our own land. You choose where you want to dwell, and I'll choose after you."

Lot chose the choicest land for himself, even though it meant he'd camp among the ungodly. When Lot went on his way, the Lord met with Abraham and proclaimed,

> Look as far as you can see in every direction—north and south, east and west. I am giving all this land, as far as you can see, to you and your descendants as a permanent possession. And I will give you so many descendants that, like the dust of the earth, they cannot be counted! Go and walk through the land in every direction, for I am giving it to you.[9]

Abraham had a healthy fear of God and a generous heart. Later, as Abraham sat outside his tent, he welcomed the three visitors. He urged them to sit and rest. He fed them a good meal and honored their presence. After one of the visitors proclaimed that Sarah would give birth to a son by this time next year, the men stood up and looked toward Sodom. The two angels started toward Sodom while the Lord lingered with Abraham.

> So the LORD told Abraham, "I have heard a great outcry from Sodom and Gomorrah, because their sin is so flagrant."[10]

What I keep wondering about this passage is, who cried out for Sodom? When Abraham interceded for the city, he asked the Lord if He'd spare the city if He found fifty, then forty, then thirty, then twenty righteous people in the town. Finally, God agreed not to destroy Sodom if even ten righteous people were found there. Unfortunately, there weren't even ten righteous people in that whole city! So who was crying out?

Could it have been Abraham's past prayers that reached God's ears? When the righteous cry out to God, He hears their prayers, and He moves with wisdom and power when the time is right.

When the angels arrived in town, they found Lot at the city gate. You can imagine his anxiety surging when he realized he was talking to men of God in the middle of a wicked and deplorable city. When the townspeople heard about the visitors, they pounded on Lot's door and demanded to have sex with them. Here's how Lot responded to the raging crowd:

> So Lot stepped outside to talk to them, shutting the door behind him. "Please, my brothers," he begged, "don't do such a wicked thing. Look, I have two virgin daughters. Let me bring them out to you, and you can do with them as you wish. But

please, leave these men alone, for they are my guests and are under my protection."[11]

Hospitality in biblical times was a high priority. But how low do you have to sink to offer your virgin daughters to a group of ravenous, depraved men to *do with as they pleased*? God, have mercy! Thankfully, the angels pulled Lot inside the house and shut the door. Then they blinded the men outside, causing confusion among them.

The angels urgently alerted Lot that God had heard the outcry and judgment was about to fall on Sodom and Gomorrah. The city was about to be destroyed. So Lot rushed to tell his daughters and their fiancés. Their response? *They thought he was only joking.* Lot had camped so long among the ungodly that he'd lost his influence and credibility.

Imagine this high-adrenaline crisis taking place on your doorstep. Everyone is screaming and yelling and adding to the chaos. Maniacal perpetrators are trying to force their way into your home. Your worst fears are coming true.

Your two unknown guests take charge. They slam the door shut, supernaturally blind the mob, and defuse the situation. You try to catch your breath. Your traumatized daughters look at you, horrified that you were about to destroy their lives. But by God's grace, He'd spared them from a life-altering trauma.

If the evil in your town was *that* palpable, and the supernatural power in your guests was *that* tangible, wouldn't you *want* to quiet your heart and listen to what they had to say?

But that's not what happened. Amid the frantic warning to get out of town, *Lot hesitated.*[12]

Lot hesitated, while Abraham interceded.

We can grow so comfortable with casual sin that we find it hard to leave behind. Instead of lingering with God because of the clarity He offers, we linger with our sin despite the confusion it brings.

When the angels told Lot to run for the hills, he again negotiated a different plan. Lot's family was so attached to their life in Sodom that Lot's wife looked back instead of running full speed ahead. She turned into a pillar of salt. The rest of Lot's earthly story is a sad commentary on a squandered life of faith.

I read this story and I'm convicted to my core. How many times have I been slow to obey or quick to negotiate? How often do we hesitate to cut and run because we want to linger with our sin a bit longer?

Dr. Warren Wiersbe offered some insight on this story:

> Abraham was the friend of God, but Lot was the friend of the world (see James 4:4), and the contrasts between these two men are easy to see. . . . Had Lot gone to Sodom because God directed him, his being there would have fulfilled divine purposes. After all, God put Joseph in Egypt, Daniel in Babylon, and Esther in Persia, and their presence turned out to be a blessing. Worldliness is not a matter of physical geography, but of heart attitude (1 John 2:15–17). *Lot's heart was in Sodom long before his body arrived there.* . . . What had happened to Lot's personal values that he would offer his daughters to satisfy the sensual appetites of a mob? (In contrast, Abraham would offer his son to the Lord). . . . Because of his faith and obedience, Abraham was a blessing to his home and to the whole world. Because of his worldliness, Lot had no spiritual influence either in the city or in his own home. . . . After

separating from Abraham, Lot had allowed his character to deteriorate, and his influence declined with it.[13]

This story makes me gasp. From the outside looking in, you'd think Lot was a poser. Pretending to believe when he was around Abraham and blending in with the world when he thought no one was watching. And as you may have noticed, we didn't even delve into the scene with Lot and his daughters.

Scripture talks about the great falling away—when those who we thought were with us abandon their faith in difficult times, proving they were never a part of us to begin with.[14] Scripture tells us that what we sow we grow, and it tells us to discern someone's life by their fruit.[15] It's one thing to discern real fruit; it's another thing to judge someone's eternal status. Is it up to *us* to decide who's in and who's out? Do we know what's going on inside every heart?

Many years ago, I read this passage from 1 Corinthians 3:12–15, and it has stuck with me ever since:

Anyone who builds on that foundation may use a variety of materials—gold, silver, jewels, wood, hay, or straw. But on the judgment day, fire will reveal what kind of work each builder has done. The fire will show if a person's work has any value. If the work survives, that builder will receive a reward. But if the work is burned up, the builder will suffer great loss. The builder will be saved, but like someone barely escaping through a wall of flames.

This passage tells us that some who are saved by grace through faith in Jesus will have very little to show for it. But if we judge them to be "unsaved," we'll be wrong. Furthermore, some fantastically play the part of a Christian but are not legitimate family members.[16] If we had only the Old Testament to go on, we might say that Lot's story came to a bitter end. But let's look at how the New Testament speaks of him.

> Later, God condemned the cities of Sodom and Gomorrah and turned them into heaps of ashes. He made them an example of what will happen to ungodly people. But God also rescued Lot out of Sodom because he was a righteous man who was sick of the shameful immorality of the wicked people around him. Yes, Lot was a righteous man who was tormented in his soul by the wickedness he saw and heard day after day. So you see, the Lord knows how to rescue godly people from their trials, even while keeping the wicked under punishment until the day of final judgment.[17]

Lot was a righteous man, tormented in his soul by the wickedness that flourished around him. Who knew?

God knew.

With laserlike precision, He sees what we cannot see. He knows what we cannot know. Lot is an example of someone who escapes as though barely escaping through the flames. God's righteousness covered Lot's sin and rescued him from judgment.

God Knows Who His Children Are

God knows who His children are. And He has not appointed us to endure His wrath—His Son already took the wrath we deserved. God has appointed us for salvation, to embrace our status as heirs, and to live a life abounding in love and fruit, with miracles all around. What a gift! We're divinely appointed for life and life abundantly!

Yes, we should discern fruit. But in our day, we've done more than discern fruit; we now harshly judge fruit. We ask questions of fellow Christians not to get to know them better but to find out where they stand. Their answer determines whether we'll validate or vilify them. What happened to Christlike compassion, soul-stirring intercession, and "there but for the grace of God go I"? We see as in a glass dimly,[18] which means we're all wrong about some things. Here are some powerful words from 1 Thessalonians 5:9–11:

> For God has not destined us, *His chosen*, to face His wrath but to be the heirs of salvation through our Lord Jesus the Anointed, *the Liberating King*, who died for us. So regardless of whether we are awake or asleep, we will live together with Him. So support one another. Keep building each other up as you have been doing. (THE VOICE)

We pride ourselves on our judgments and astute assessments, but we simply don't know what we do not know. Some of our brothers and sisters have solid saving faith in Jesus Christ but may see things differently than you do. Their interpretation and reaction to current events may be as wrong as the day is long. But does God know how to correct and direct His children? Does He know where we're blind? Does He see our tendency to judge others through the lens of our strengths while we justify our weaknesses? Yes! And do our shortcomings and blind spots disqualify us from the kingdom? No. Never. Not ever.

That's not to say our opinions and reactions don't matter; they do. Compare Abraham's and Lot's lives for a clear example of both a fruitful and "barely saved" life. Anything the world has to offer is a shabby counterfeit compared to the beauty and the wonder of truly knowing and walking with our Maker. Our heavenly Father deserves our highest praise, best offerings, and wholehearted trust. He is our best thing. Always and forever. And one day, when we see Him face-to-face, we may, for the briefest moment, wish we'd lived like His promises were true, because they are.

God loves His children, and He's not at all unclear about who belongs to the family and who does not.

I pray Lot's story encourages you, especially if you have loved ones who were raised in the faith but have camped among the ungodly. Your cry reaches God's ears. He can penetrate their hearts. You may see no evidence of trust from your perspective, but if it's in there, God sees, God knows, and He'll activate their spiritual root system at just the right time. He'll go to great lengths to rescue them because He loves them.

He'll Get You Safely Home

Though the road to salvation is narrow, the love of God runs deep and wide. True, there's only one way to the Father, and that's through His Son, Jesus Christ.[19] But it's also true that we may find ourselves utterly surprised on judgment day when we find out who's there and who's not.

Some of God's precious children will cross the finish line

still tempted by their addictions (until they see Jesus). Others will stumble over the finish line, burned out and stressed out (until they see Jesus). On that great day when Jesus returns, He'll find mature and immature believers, selfless and selfish believers, those full of faith and those still battling fear. Those who lingered long hours with Him and those who, like Lot, lingered too long with the world. But when we finally see Him, we will be like Him, for we shall see Him as He is.[20]

We're saved by grace and sealed by the Holy Spirit. And we're all in different places on our journey. But God knows our names. He knows about our faith and our fruit. Nothing is hidden from Him. Every one of us is sometimes a pile of contradictions, yet He still lavishly loves us and is proud to call us His own. It's grace that has saved us. The Spirit that has sealed us. And faith that changes us.

Now all glory to God, who is able to keep you from falling away and will bring you with great joy into his glorious presence without a single fault. All glory to him who alone is God, our Savior through Jesus Christ our Lord. All glory, majesty, power, and authority are his before all time, and in the present, and beyond all time! Amen.

JUDE VV. 24–25

Isn't the good news the best news ever? Doesn't the reality of God's grace compel you to worship your King? Draw near to God. Bow low before Him. Surrender every area of your life to Him. Tell Him He's your King. Your Lord. Your Father. And your Righteous Judge. He's your Healer. Your Defender. Your Banner. And your Strong Tower.

Draw near to Him. Invite Him to work wonders in your life. Listen for His voice. Do what He says. And trust Him when you can't see, sense, or hear Him. He's with you even now. And He's committed to leading you every step of the way until you're safely home.

Reflect

1. Read Malachi 3:6–7 and consider God's appeal for His children to draw near only to have some respond this way: "How can we return when we have never gone away?" Write down your thoughts about that exchange.

2. Read Psalm 106:24–25 and consider the glorious promises written over God's chosen people. Yet they refused to believe His promises were true. How did they respond? Write down their response and a modern-day example of what it looks like to reject God's promises and thus stay in the smallness of your circumstances.

3. Read 2 Peter 1:1–10. Write down the verses that stand out to you and what you sense God is saying to you through this passage.

4. Go back to the book of Malachi and read Malachi 3:16–18. Though the lines on earth may seem blurry regarding who

walks with God and who doesn't, there's perfect clarity in heaven. Write out this passage and make it a paraphrased prayer.

Pray

High King of Heaven, Lord, God Almighty, I bow before Your throne, and I worship You alone.

There is no God like You, Lord! You alone created the heavens and the earth. And You alone are returning one day for Your people. Awaken me to the wonders of Your love. I want to remember what You remember and forget what You've chosen to forget. Remove every memory of trauma, offense, and betrayal. Remind me what a walking miracle I am! Refresh my memory of all the times You healed, restored, and defended my honor. I can trust You. Help me change the way I think, the things I remember, and the promises I need to ponder. Renew my mind in such a miraculous way that it completely changes my life. You remembered me when You hung on that cross. May I remember You, think of You, and ponder Your goodness all the days of my life. May I walk so intimately with You, so in step with You, that when others encounter me, they encounter You. Grow me from strength to strength, glory to glory, that I might shine ever brighter until the full light of day. In Jesus' precious name I pray, amen.

Respond

Light a candle. Put on some instrumental music. Grab your Bible and a journal (and a warm blanket if you'd like). Prayerfully page through the Gospels and find a story that stands out to you. Imagine yourself in the crowd of onlookers. What do you notice about Jesus? What do you love about Him? Tell Him so now.

Continue to linger with God. Ponder the ways He's provided for you. Think back to the times you didn't think you'd make it through, but you did, by His grace. Remember His goodness and thank Him for it.

Linger with God and thank Him for some of the amazing people who have crossed your path over the years. Name them by name and then praise His name!

Ask God to help you forget what you need to forget and to remember what you need to remember. Then make a habit of remembering redemptively.

Ponder His Presence

What Does It Mean to Fear God?

My husband Kev is six-foot-three and about 250 pounds. He's a sizable oak of righteousness. Our three grown sons now stand shoulder to shoulder with him. But when they were young, they thought he was a giant. Kev is patient, kind, funny, and *so* sturdy. He's consistently steady and rarely loses his cool. Our boys felt safe in his care. They never had to worry about moodiness, fits of rage, or inconsistent reactions. But they also had a healthy respect for him. If Dad stepped in and said, "Enough!" they knew he meant it.

Some believe that the fear of the Lord is an Old Testament concept, but I highly disagree.

Let the whole world fear the Lord, and let everyone stand in awe of him.[1]

The Bible says that the Son is the radiance of God's glory. He's the exact representation of God.[2] Jesus came to earth to save us. This should inspire *more* reverent awe in us, not less. Wouldn't you say?

We often misunderstand the kind of fear Scripture talks about, which is rightly fearing God.

> There is no fear in love. But perfect love drives out fear, because fear has to do with punishment. The one who fears is not made perfect in love.[3]

The fear in this passage speaks of phobias, terror, dread, and a cowering sense that you don't know what's coming at you. Think of a cowering child at the hands of a reactive, abusive father. Our God is a good Father. And a fantastic communicator. He hates what will destroy you and loves what will establish you. He's highly protective of you and is never given to fits of rage or inconsistent overreactions.

> You see, you have not received a spirit that returns you to slavery, so you have nothing to fear. The Spirit you have received adopts you *and welcomes you* into God's own family. That's why we call out to Him, "Abba! Father!" *as we would address a loving daddy.*[4]

The more we learn to trust God's love, the more we'll understand why He deserves all the honor and glory and power forever. He never misuses His power.

> The fear of the LORD is the beginning of wisdom, and knowledge of the Holy One is understanding.[5]

The fear in the Proverbs passage speaks of reverential awe. The word *terror* is also used in this description, but that fits when you read stories in Scripture of when God invades our earthly existence.

For instance, when the two Marys at the tomb saw the angel, they saw his appearance as lightning, and his clothes were white as snow. The earth quaked in his presence. Wouldn't that terrify you? These dear women were scared until God comforted them. Then they were excited. Meanwhile, the big, strong guards were sprawled out like dead men.[6]

Let's conclude with one more verse.

For God has not given us a spirit of fear, but of power and of love and of a sound mind.[7]

The word "fear" in this passage speaks of timidity or cowardice. God has not given us the spirit of a coward. He's empowered us with His very Spirit, which works in and through us with power, love, and a sound mind.

We've only scratched the surface of what it means to live in awe of God. I would say that to the degree we reverently honor Him will be the degree that we come to really know Him.

Prayer

High King of Heaven, I honor You this day. May Your kingdom come, Your will be done, on earth, in me, as it is in heaven. I love You, Lord. Amen.

Then he added, "Pay close attention to what you hear. The closer you listen, the more understanding you will be given—and you will receive even more. To those who listen to my teaching, more understanding will be given. But for those who are not listening, even what little understanding they have will be taken away from them."

MARK 4:24–25

Acknowledgments

Though my name is on the cover of this book, I could not have finished this project without the help of friends, family, and colleagues.

Kyle Olund, I'm so grateful to serve with you. You're an amazing man of God, an insightful friend, and a wise editor.

To Damon Reiss, Caren Wolfe, Ashley Reed, Elizabeth Hawkins, Madison Baird, Lauren Ash, and the rest of the W team. I'm so honored to serve alongside you.

To Jennifer Stair. You had your hands full with this one, and you did a brilliant job. Richest blessings to Brooke Hill and Kit Tosello. Thank you for setting the bar high. You brought excellence to this message. Thank you!

Steve Laube, thank you for your faithfulness through the years.

To my Marvel Prayer Warrior Women, Esther, Karna, and Melissa. I met my match when I started praying with you. Your fierce, focused, passionate prayers and loving friendship have changed my life. I'm forever grateful.

To Lynn. Kev and I love and appreciate you more than we can ever express. Thank you for your constant and continual intercession. You're a trusted voice in our lives.

To the team at Faith Radio. What an honor it is to serve alongside you. Here's to many more faithful, fruitful years of service!

To our Rwandan family. You've shown us what kingdom life looks like. You inspire us, challenge us, and encourage us. May God continue to use you to change the world. We love and appreciate you so!

To our wild and wonderful extended family (Mom, siblings, in-laws, nephews, nieces). I cannot imagine life without you. Love you more than I can say. You're my happy place.

To Jake, Lizzie, Luke, Kristen, Jordan, Jiethyl, and all our grandbabies. You are my world! I love you to the moon and back. May all your dreams come true. May God's love feel more tangible with each passing day. And may He continue to use our family to help as many people as possible. I love that we have each other.

To Kev, my best thing. I don't want to make a move without you. I praise God for all He's done in and through us. May He continue to work wonders in and through us. And may He continue to surprise us with His goodness.

To Jesus. My life is wrapped up in Yours. Thank You for saving, healing, and redeeming me in ways I never thought possible. I'm living expectant for Your soon return. Please breathe life into the words on these pages. Heal broken hearts. Set captives free. Bring prodigals home. And awaken us all to the wonder of Your great love. Amen.

About the Author

S usie Larson is a bestselling author, national speaker, and host of the popular radio show Susie Larson Live. Whether behind a desk or behind a mic, Susie lives out her passion to see people everywhere awakened to the depth of God's love, the value of their soul, and the height of their calling in Christ Jesus.

A two-time finalist for the prestigious John C. Maxwell Transformational Leadership Award, Susie is the author of over 20 books and devotionals, and her Daily Blessings reach over half a million people each week on social media. Her radio show is heard daily on the Faith Radio Network, as well as around the world through her podcast, which has more than 3.5 million downloads. A popular media guest and guest host, Susie has frequently appeared on shows like Focus on the Family, Life Today, and Family Life Today.

In addition to her work and ministry, Susie loves to laugh and relax with her family. She and her husband, Kevin, have been married since 1985. Together they have three wonderful (and hilarious) sons, three beautiful daughters-in-law, a growing bunch of delightful grandchildren, and one adorable pit bull named Memphis.

Notes

Introduction
1. Psalm 23:4.
2. Matthew 10:30.
3. Zephaniah 3:17.
4. Isaiah 55:9.
5. Hebrews 4:16.
6. Romans 8:28.
7. Psalm 16:11 NKJV.
8. Isaiah 55:8–9.
9. Matthew 17:1–6.
10. John 18:1–6.
11. Psalm 73:26.

Chapter 1
1. Mark 1:18.
2. Mark 14:66–72.
3. John 21:15–17.
4. John 20:1–2.
5. John 13:23; 21:20.
6. John 20:4.
7. John 20:8.
8. John 20:8–9.
9. John 20:11–13.
10. John 20:13.
11. John 20:19.
12. Luke 19:10.
13. Jesus and the Samaritan woman (John 4); Jesus interrupted

a funeral (Luke 7); Jesus healed a Roman soldier's servant (Matthew 8); Jesus raised Lazarus from the dead (John 11); Jesus appeared to His followers after His death (1 Corinthians 15:6 and other passages); Jesus healed a demon-possessed boy (Mark 9); Jesus delivered the demoniac (Mark 5).

14. John 20:21–22.
15. John 20:28.
16. John 20:29.
17. John 20:29, Interlinear Bible Search, https://www.studylight.org /lexicons/eng/greek/3107.html.
18. 1 John 2:1.
19. The original word for "life" in this verse is *zoe*, which translates this way: "The absolute fullness of life, both ethical and essential, which belongs to God . . . life real and genuine, a life active and vigorous, devoted to God, blessed, in the portion even in this world of those who put their trust in Christ, but after the resurrection to be consummated by new accessions (among them a more perfect body), and to last forever." In other words, John 20:30–31 could be translated this way: "The disciples saw Jesus do many other miraculous signs in addition to the ones recorded in this book. But these are written so that you may continue to believe that Jesus is the Messiah, the Son of God, and that by believing in him you will have *life* by the power of his name—*life real and genuine, active and vigorous, full of hope for today and promise for tomorrow.*" The miracles of God, the presence of God, changes everything. John 20:31, Interlinear Bible Search, StudyLight.org.
20. Matthew 6:10.

Ponder His Presence: If I Chase the Sensational, Might I Miss the Supernatural?

1. Gerald Fry, NIV *New Spirit-Filled Life Bible: Kingdom Equipping Through the Power of the Word* (Nashville: Thomas Nelson, 2002), 1688–89.
2. Philippians 3:16.

Chapter 2

1. Psalm 19:2 NIV.
2. Romans 2:11.
3. A.W. Tozer, *The Pursuit of God: A 31-Day Experience* (Camp Hill, PA: Christian Publications, Inc., 1995), 98–99.
4. James 4:8.
5. Hebrews 12:1.
6. 2 Corinthians 4:17–18.
7. Psalm 33:6–9.
8. Psalm 8:4 NKJV.
9. Lamentations 3:22–25 NIV.
10. Psalm 46:1 NKJV, emphasis added.
11. Elizabeth Barrett Browning, *Aurora Leigh* (New York, NY: Oxford University Press, 2008), 246.
12. Chip Ingram, *Discover Your True Self: How to Silence the Lies of Your Past and Actually Experience Who God Says You Are* (Grand Rapids, MI: Baker Books, 2020), 102.
13. Mark Batterson, *Whisper: How to Hear the Voice of God* (Colorado Springs, CO: Multnomah, 2017), 16–17.

Ponder His Presence: What Does It Mean to Quench the Holy Spirit?

1. 1 Thessalonians 5:19, https://www.studylight.org/lexicons/eng/greek/4570.html.
2. NIV *New Spirit-Filled Life Bible*, 1688.

Chapter 3

1. Galatians 5:22–23.
2. John 15:5.
3. Jeremiah 17:5–6 NKJV.
4. Blessed (*bawrak*)–Bless yourself, cause to kneel Trust–To be bold, secure, and confident; to feel safe and be carefree. Hope and confidence–Act of confiding; security; the object of confidence. Jeremiah 17:7–8, https://www.studylight.org/lexicons/eng/hebrew/01288.html.

5. Jeremiah 17:7–8.

6. John 2:4.

7. John 2:5.

8. Hosea 2:23; Isaiah 42:6.

9. *New Living Translation Study Bible* (Carol Stream, IL: Tyndale, 2004), 2124–25.

10. To read the story of the woman with the issue of blood, see Matthew 9:20–22, Mark 5:25–34, and Luke 8:43–48.

11. This quote is widely attributed to Martin Luther.

12. Read Ruth's amazing story in the book of Ruth; Esther's incredible story in the book of Esther; Deborah's story in Judges 4–5; Mary's story in the Gospels of Matthew, Mark, Luke, and John; the Samaritan woman's story in John 4:4–30; and the Syrophoenician woman's story in Matthew 15:21–28.

Ponder His Presence: How Do I Know If I'm Hearing the Voice of God?

1. John 10:25–30.

2. Matthew 5:8.

3. Proverbs 2:10.

4. Oswald Chambers, *My Utmost for His Highest*, August 13, https://utmost.org/do-not-quench-the-spirit/.

Chapter 4

1. Psalm 77:10–14.

2. Exodus 3:4–6.

3. A.W. Tozer, *Knowledge of the Holy* (San Francisco: Harper and Row, 1961), viii.

4. Revelation 1:8.

Ponder His Presence: How Should God's Presence Impact Us?

1. Matthew 17:2–6.

2. John 18:4–6.

3. Philippians 2:10–11.

Chapter 5

1. Ephesians 2:8–9.

2. 2 Corinthians 9:8 NKJV.

3. 2 Corinthians 9:8, StudyLight.org.

4. Romans 5:20–21.

5. Galatians 5:4.

6. John Lindell, *Soul Set Free: Why Grace Is More Liberating Than You Believe* (Lake Mary, FL: Charisma House, 2019), 6–7.

7. John 1:16–18.

8. Ephesians 2:8–9.

9. Psalm 139:23–24.

10. Psalm 19:12–14.

Ponder His Presence: Is Feeling Good the Same As Feeling God?

1. James 1:17.

2. James 4:8.

Chapter 6

1. This is my paraphrase of what Maria said.

2. Max Lucado, *Glory Days: Living Your Promised Land Life Now* (Nashville: Thomas Nelson, 2015), 148.

3. Ephesians 2:8–10.

4. Hebrews 12:1–3.

5. Psalm 18:1–19.

6. Psalm 40:1–3.

7. Isaiah 40:31, 53:5; Psalm 23:1–3, 107:20; 1 Peter 2:24.

8. Isaiah 41:10; Psalm 34:4–7; 1 Peter 5:7; 2 Timothy 1:7.

9. Psalm 4:8, 121:3–4, 127:2.

10. Ephesians 2:10; 1 John 4:16.

11. Psalm 23:4–6; Romans 8:31–39.
12. Luke 6:38; Philippians 4:19.
13. Psalm 46:10.
14. Psalm 127:3–5, 128; Isaiah 43:5–7, 44:3–4; 1 Corinthians 13:4–7; Ephesians 3:20–21.
15. Psalm 37; 75:10.
16. Mark 16:17–18; 1 Corinthians 4:20; 1 Peter 4:11.
17. This is my paraphrase from my conversation with Dr. Allender regarding his book *Redeeming Heartache: How Past Suffering Reveals Our True Calling* (Grand Rapids, MI: Zondervan, 2021).

Ponder His Presence: What Does It Mean to Grieve the Holy Spirit?

1. Matthew 18:20.
2. R.T. Kendall, *The Sensitivity of the Spirit* (Lake Mary, FL: Charisma House, 2002), 4.

Chapter 7

1. Romans 8:31–39.
2. James 4:7.
3. For more on this topic, check out my book *Strong in Battle: Why the Humble Will Prevail* (Grand Rapids, MI: Bethany House, 2022).
4. Pete Greig, *How to Hear God: A Simple Guide for Normal People* (Grand Rapids, MI: Zondervan, 2022), 20–21.
5. Psalm 113:5–6.
6. Psalm 138:6.
7. Psalm 138:6, https://www.studylight.org/lexicons/eng/hebrew/03045.html.
8. Romans 8:28.

Ponder His Presence: Is There Anything I Can Do When God Seems Silent?

1. 2 Corinthians 1:20.
2. Exodus 32:1 NIV.

Chapter 8

1. Acts 3:19 THE VOICE.
2. Luke 15:31–32.
3. 1 Peter 2:5, 9–10.
4. Hebrews 6:1.
5. Luke 8:14–15.
6. Colossians 2:6–7.
7. John Eldredge, *Resilient: Restoring Your Weary Soul in These Turbulent Times* (Nashville: Thomas Nelson, 2022), 199.
8. Hebrews 6:9–12.
9. John 15:8.
10. NLT *Life Application Study Bible* (Grand Rapids, MI: Tyndale, 1996, 2004, 2007), 1236.
11. Jeremiah 17:7.
12. Acts 17:24–25.

Ponder His Presence: If God Can Intervene, Why Doesn't He?

1. John 16:7.
2. Matthew 11:6 NKJV.

Chapter 9

1. Acts 22:3–5.
2. Acts 22:6–10.
3. 1 Corinthians 9:24–27 AMP.
4. 1 Corinthians 6:20.
5. C.S. Lewis, *The Essential C.S. Lewis* (New York: Simon & Schuster, 1996), 362.
6. Luke 19:10.
7. Proverbs 19:17.
8. 2 Peter 3:9.
9. Philippians 4:19.
10. Trust: A firm belief in the reliability, truth, ability, or strength of someone. Entrust: To assign responsibility for doing

something. *Oxford English Dictionary Online*, s.v. "trust"; s.v. "entrust," oed.com.

Ponder His Presence: What Does It Mean to Fix Our Eyes on What We Cannot See?

1. 2 Corinthians 4:17–18.
2. 2 Corinthians 4:17–18, StudyLight.org.
3. Ephesians 1:17–21 NIV.

Chapter 10

1. Genesis 16:2.
2. Romans 8:28.
3. Genesis 16:4–5.
4. Genesis 17:5.
5. Hebrews 11:1–2, 8–12.
6. Revelation 22:12.
7. Saundra Dalton-Smith, *Sacred Rest: Recover Your Life, Renew Your Energy, Restore Your Sanity* (Nashville: FaithWords, 2017), 151.
8. John 15:16–17.
9. Genesis 13:14–17.
10. Genesis 18:20.
11. Genesis 19:6–8.
12. Genesis 19:16.
13. Warren Wiersbe, *The Wiersbe Bible Commentary* (Colorado Springs, CO: David C. Cook, 2007), 78.
14. 1 John 2:19.
15. Matthew 7:16.
16. Matthew 7:21–23.
17. 2 Peter 2:6–9.
18. 1 Corinthians 13:12.
19. John 14:6.
20. 1 John 3:1–2.

Ponder His Presence: What Does It Mean to Fear God?

1. Psalm 33:8.
2. Hebrews 1:3.
3. 1 John 4:18 NIV.
4. Romans 8:15 THE VOICE.
5. Proverbs 9:10 NIV.
6. Matthew 28.
7. 2 Timothy 1:7 NKJV.

From the Publisher

GREAT BOOKS

ARE EVEN BETTER WHEN THEY'RE SHARED!

Help other readers find this one:

- Post a review at your favorite online bookseller

- Post a picture on a social media account and share why you enjoyed it

- Send a note to a friend who would also love it—or better yet, give them a copy

Thanks for reading!